CREATING

A LIFE OF JOY

CREATING

A LIFE OF JOY

A MEDITATIVE GUIDE

SALLE MERRILL REDFIELD

WARNER BOOKS

A Time Warner Company

I would like to gratefully acknowledge the following authors and publishers who have granted permission to use excerpts from the following works:

Information on the six human needs by Anthony Robbins © Anthony Robbins Companies. Reprinted by permission.

From *Cancer as a Turning Point* by Lawrence LeShawn. Copyright © 1989 by Lawrence LeShawn, Ph.D. Used by permission of Dutton, a division of Penguin Putnam, Inc.

Copyright information continued on page 143.

Warner Books, Inc., 1271 Avenue of the Americas, New York, NY 10020
Visit our Web site at www.twbookmark.com

 A Time Warner Company

Printed in the United States of America
First Printing: December 1999
10 9 8 7 6 5 4 3 2 1

Library of Congress Cataloging-in-Publication Data

Redfield, Salle Merrill.
    Creating a life of joy : a meditative guide / Salle Merrill Redfield.
        p.   cm.
    ISBN 0-446-67587-3
    1. Joy.   2. Meditations.   3. Conduct of life.   I. Title.
BJ1481.R43   1999
158.1'2—dc21   99-17005
                                                                          CIP

Cover design by Carolyn Lechter
Cover art by Honi Werner
Book design by L & G McRee

For my husband,

James Fulton Redfield,

a true friend and a real sweetheart

My heartfelt thanks to the following: John Winthrop Austin for never saying no all the times I asked for one more piece of research; my mother, Lulu Richardson, for her editing comments; my dear friend Savann Sherrill, whose ideas are intermingled with mine throughout this book; Larry Kirshbaum and Joann Davis for creating an avenue for my work; and most of all to my editor, Claire Zion, for her skillful editorial touch.

Contents

Foreword

As we enter the new millennium, we seem to be doing so with a new sense of what life is about. If once we reduced our lives to a mere series of challenges—coming of age, finding a way to make a living, marrying and being good parents, getting our children through school, finding a way to retire, and facing death— we are now envisioning an existence almost unlimited in its possibilities for creativity and actualization. This new picture of "the good life" has been developing for many decades, arising out of the best of our religious traditions, the current research on highly creative individuals, and the recent interest in spirituality and prayer.

We know now that the idea of psychological growth—getting past all the things that hold us back and entering a state of mind that unleashes our best selves—is a real thing, and a step that everyone who wants to live fully must take.

Remarkable people have discernible traits in common, and it is no accident. At this point in history the process each of us must go through to recognize and cultivate these traits is clear. All that remains is for each of us to believe, to know that a better, more joyful life exists, and that such a life can be consciously created.

Key is the power of our own intention, that focus of mind that expects great things to happen. In the following pages, Salle explores how to use the mind to first understand our limiting habits and then to move through them, step by step, to find and actualize the personal dream that is our spiritual birthright.

When strong intention is combined with regular meditation, something magic begins to happen. We hear our inner voice, that intuitive faculty that serves to guide us through difficult times and toward our goals.

The fact is, we don't have to go through life alone, thinking we have to intellectually figure out every decision and course of action. There is within us, once we clear ourselves of the chatter in our lives, a higher knowing that helps us chart a truer course. All we have to do is decide to stop and listen, and to embrace this knowledge as our own.

Emerging is the secret of a joyous "good life." In the new millennium it will be common knowledge.

—James Redfield

Joy is the holy fire that keeps our purpose warm
and our intelligence aglow.

—HELEN KELLER

CHAPTER ONE

Preparing for Joy

W̲e are all capable of living lives characterized by great joy. Within each of us is an amazing human spirit that is strong enough to overcome pain and disappointment. And no matter what our current situation happens to be, or what beliefs we may currently harbor about ourselves, we can tap into that inner strength and wisdom and move forward to create more joy.

At times we diminish our ability to experience joy by being preoccupied with the past. When we do this, we allow what took place ten or twenty years ago to influence our lives more than what's currently happening. A disturbing childhood event can leave us frozen with doubt and fear. We may begin to believe consciously or unconsciously that we are either unable to have a happy life or are unworthy of having one. But these experiences can be transcended, opening us to a whole new level of joy.

Someone going through a divorce or a relationship breakup may think, "My life is ruined. I'll never be happy because she left me." He focuses more on his loss than on building a new life for himself. Anyone who has ever ended a relationship only to later enter into a better one knows that time heals this wound. The popular singer Garth Brooks expresses this idea beautifully in the song "Unanswered Prayers." In this song Brooks sings about running into his high school sweetheart and realizing how grateful he was that the relationship didn't work out. At the time it ended he felt pain about the loss. Since the breakup, however, he married a woman he truly loved, and because of all the love in this marriage he realized that the breakup was actually a blessing. The song serves as a reminder that sometimes when a prayer isn't answered, it is because there is something better in store for us. This is not to diminish the discomfort of a relationship ending. It can be painful and it takes time to heal. But it doesn't have to stop us from moving on and experiencing love again.

Financial strains and physical concerns can also leave us with little energy to create lives of joy. In such cases, the present situation can make us feel stuck and unable to move forward. Here it is very important to avoid the belief that our problems are somehow different from the problems other people have faced and are therefore unchangeable or special. Regardless of

our situation, someone somewhere has already faced a similar set of circumstances and found a way to bring joy back into his or her life.

The fact is that none of us are entirely alone, facing insurmountable problems. There is always a light at the end of the tunnel. Most successful people have suffered disappointments and setbacks, if not utter failure. And everyone has had loss. It seems to come with the territory of being human. What also comes with the human condition is the ability to prevail over any challenge and to use our experiences for personal growth. For a while we may feel hopeless and unsure of what to do, but eventually we can find the strength and wisdom to use the experience for our highest good.

One person who has learned to use his experience to grow is a man I know named Jerry. To meet him, you would think he had lived a charmed life. He is strong, healthy, and always upbeat. Daily he concentrates on what he can do to make his dreams come true. Jerry faced the challenges of being a prisoner during the Korean War, having to learn to walk a second time after an injury, losing one home to an earthquake and another to a fire. He also lost a successful business due to a negligent business partner. Numerous tragedies have dotted his sixty-something years, yet Jerry still has a great belief in the miracle of life. His focus is on actualizing his goals and making others happy. When I call him and say, "Jerry, how are you?" his response is always, "If I were any better, I couldn't stand it."

I also know a woman named Gloria who has a deep love for life, even though she and her husband, Bob, lost their adult son to AIDS. They cared for him in their home the last two years of his life. It wasn't the first time she had faced tragedy. At another point in her life Gloria had been homeless and unable to care for her children because of her addiction to alcohol. She overcame her addiction and dedicated her life to helping others in similar situations. Gloria is a beautiful woman with an infectious laugh and a wonderful sense of humor. You never hear her lamenting her past. She is always focusing on her strong spiritual beliefs and how she can help someone in the present moment.

Neither Jerry nor Gloria has had an ideal life, yet both are purposeful and optimistic. They are good reminders that growing from painful experiences and living in the present moment are how we find joy and happiness.

Our Needs

There comes a point in each of our lives when we realize that we are responsible for our own joy. Long-lasting happiness can't come from another person or material possessions. We may enjoy being around people and developing rich relationships, and we can find short-term pleasure in a new car, house, or computer. After a while, though, we take things for granted. Our

possessions don't shine as brightly as they did when we first acquired them. And the people we are closest to will sometimes
disagree with us or need to focus their attention elsewhere.

Having the day-to-day joy we long for comes from understanding our basic human needs and developing ways to meet
them. Abraham Maslow, a founder of modern humanistic psychology, has theorized that we have certain primary desires that
must be satisfied in order for us to flourish. Maslow constructed
a basic hierarchy of needs that many theorists have acknowledged and built upon. This hierarchy ranges from the basic
need for food and shelter all the way to the higher need for purpose and self-actualization.

Anthony Robbins, author of *Awaken the Giant Within*, is a con-
temporary author who offers a classification of higher need that
I find helpful. He talks about six human needs that people continuously seek to meet either consciously or unconsciously as
they strive to survive and function at various levels of personal
development in the world: certainty, uncertainty/variety, significance, connection, growth, and contribution.

In our need to have certainty in our lives, we pursue our basic
physiological needs as well as a stable environment of peace,
love, and joy. We pursue our need for uncertainty through variety, surprise, and small challenges. Our need for significance is
met when we are recognized and appreciated by others and acknowledged for our contributions. Connection comes from loving others, being loved, and feeling a sense of belonging. This

includes a connection to God or the divine source of all that is the universe. The need to grow is met by traditional education, individual exploration, and study, and most of all through life experiences. And the need to make a contribution and leave a legacy is fulfilled by finding work that has purpose, volunteering our time, tithing our money, and parenting our children.

Certain activities meet a variety of our needs. A man can take his family on a vacation and feel a sense of significance by paying for the vacation, connection from being with people he loves, variety or uncertainty because he is visiting a new place, and growth because he will learn about the local culture.

As simple as these needs are, the challenge comes when we try to find our unique style for meeting them in positive ways. The need for significance could be met by becoming the president of a major company or by joining a gang and carrying a gun. For some people, abusing alcohol and using drugs temporarily meets the need for connection with others. Someone might feel certainty because the drug makes him feel better, at least for a while. And he gains significance because being drunk or high enables him to delude himself into feeling more self-esteem. This is one of the challenges of these addictions. They can seem to meet so many of a person's needs. Often we are hooked before we realize that the alcohol or drug's ability to meet our needs is just an illusion.

The same idea applies to food. We can be certain that a little comfort food during times of stress will make us feel better, and there is an endless variety of foods to eat. Just look at all the ice cream flavors on the market. We get connection because we can be with friends while dining out. And significance comes in when someone eats only at the most popular restaurants or drinks only the best wines. We can also get significance by having the reputation of baking the best apple pie in our community. Food can be one of the greatest pleasures in life. It can also lead to obesity, disease, and various eating disorders if it becomes our only method of meeting our needs.

This is why learning to meet our needs consciously is so important. If we have a pattern of meeting our needs in destructive ways, we have to be wary. We need to learn to first understand which needs are being met by our destructive behavior and then look for another way to meet them. The same needs that we have seemed to satisfy through the abuse of food, alcohol, shopping, or sex can be met in a healthier, more productive manner.

Become an expert at recognizing how you are meeting your needs. If there is something you love to do, notice which needs are getting met. If there are activities you have to do but don't like, look closely at your reaction and notice which needs are not being met.

Beliefs About Life

I once attended a women's retreat where I met an elegant older woman named Ellen, who radiated optimism. At seventy she was graceful and refreshing to be around. On the last day of the retreat she and I took an early morning walk. As we walked, I questioned her about her optimism. "Ellen, have you always been this joyous about life?" I asked. Her immediate response was, "Oh, no, I used to be a very depressed person." A bit surprised by her answer, I asked her to tell me more. She described how she had once been a magazine editor in New York, always in a hurry, living by everyone else's standards, and never having an original thought or action. She came home from work one day and discovered that her husband of thirty-seven years had left her. She was shattered.

Her children became so worried about her that they insisted she take a trip to Hawaii to visit her college roommate. While there she did some soul-searching and came to several life-changing conclusions. I asked her what her greatest realization was, and she said, "I learned I had to accept life on life's terms and that the only things I really have control over in life are my actions and my ability to interpret events. If something happens to me that is painful, I have the choice to use it or allow it to devastate me."

She went on to tell me that her first trip to Hawaii ended up being so healing that she stayed an entire month. During her stay she coincidentally heard about a class that helped people understand their beliefs about life. Through the class she realized how many of her beliefs were either unrealistic or belonged to her deceased parents and her ex-husband. She also realized that her expectations for herself and others were sometimes too rigid. She was trying to live up to what everyone else said was best for her, which made her depressed and hard to be around at times. Once she changed her beliefs about herself and others, she began to smile more and enjoy life.

As we ended our walk, she turned to me and said, "Salle, this is my real secret to being a joyful person: I make my life easy. I spend more time being grateful for what I have instead of focusing on what isn't working. I no longer believe that people have to do things my way and that I have to be perfect."

Ellen used her divorce as a cosmic push to examine her beliefs about life. Fortunately we don't need a crisis to prod us into examining our beliefs and changing them when needed. Anytime we feel unrest or the simple desire to change our lives for the better, we can explore our beliefs.

Early in life we are taught to live according to the standards of others. Our parents as well as family members, the media, and people in the community influenced how we viewed the world. Appropriate behavior was understood quickly. And in order to be accepted and fit in, we acted a certain way.

If we hold the belief that "I can only be happy when life is the way I expect it to be and people treat me the way I want them to," we are setting ourselves up for disappointment. Or if we believe we can only be happy when we have the perfect body, a fabulous job, and a house in the most prestigious neighborhood, we will regularly wake up frustrated.

There are many factors in life that we can't control. The world is forever changing. Homes become disorganized when there are children and hectic schedules. The weather doesn't always cooperate with our plans. And relationships cycle through the push/pull of doing things together and needing individual space. It becomes a waste of time and energy to hold ourselves and others up to perfectionistic standards that are based on a television program we saw or a book we read, or our own imagination.

For instance, I once heard a man talk about how he felt like a failure, even though he had an annual income of a million dollars and was working at his ideal occupation. This man was extremely unhappy, even though he had a wife who loved him dearly and was expecting their first child. He was in perfect health and living in a beautiful home overlooking the ocean. He was miserable because he believed he should be achieving more. In his mind he had failed to live up to his expectations and the expectations of his parents. He also had a belief that in order to succeed in life he must be serious all the time. Laughter was out. And he felt that he couldn't spend his weekends enjoying his favorite hobby, surfing, because that didn't fit into his image of being a father and a successful businessman.

Fortunately he explored his beliefs about life and realized that he was being too hard on himself. His wife was supportive of his love of surfing. And his parents were extremely proud of him. He adopted new beliefs that allowed him to relax and be grateful for all the blessings in his life.

This man's behavior may seem strange to someone who will never make a million dollars a year, yet we all behave this way on some level. We compare ourselves to others and think we aren't very successful, even though we have accomplished many things since the day we were born.

We may believe we don't have anything special to offer the world because someone in our childhood told us we didn't matter. Or we think we have to behave according to some hypothetical standard in order to be a good parent, businessperson, or community leader. Beliefs like these can create tremendous stress and prevent us from living lives full of inner peace and joy.

If you feel you limit yourself because of certain unconscious or outdated beliefs, take time to explore your beliefs and how they originated. Maybe when you were a child you heard someone make a passing remark about how women or men were supposed to behave. As a child you didn't have the ability to question the remark. You might have accepted it as truth. But

11

now that you are older, you have the ability to form your own opinions.

To discover your beliefs, ask yourself questions like "What do I believe about money?" or "What needs to happen in order for me to be joyful?" Tailor these questions to any area of your life. And if you discover a belief that no longer serves you, replace it with a new belief.

Find a role model that lives life the way you want to and question his or her beliefs, if possible. Or imagine yourself being extremely joyful and ask yourself what types of beliefs you would hold about living life fully. This will give you an idea of new beliefs to adopt. Also practice having more fun and laughter in your life. This will shake out any old beliefs that say life has to be serious or all work.

Learn to play more. Relax and lighten up. Try new things. Connect with the beauty of the world. Make each day special. And, most of all, take time to be appreciative of your many assets. This will guarantee you more joyful beliefs and experiences in life.

❧

Meditation

The following meditation is designed to help you prepare for more joy in your life.

When doing the meditation, read each line or paragraph as a complete thought before moving on to the next line. Trust the thoughts that come, and make sure you take the time you need between questions. You might find it helpful to read a line or paragraph and then close your eyes and visualize what you've read. Or you may want to tape-record the meditation using your own voice and then play it back to yourself.

When you are ready to begin, go to a quiet, comfortable place where you won't be interrupted for about fifteen minutes.

You might find it helpful to have a pen and paper ready so that after the meditation you can write down any ideas that come to you.

As we begin the meditation, move around slightly until you are in a comfortable position . . .

Lower your shoulders and relax your hands and feet . . .

Now take a deep breath and count to five before releasing it . . .

Take another deep breath and feel your body releasing any tension as you breathe out . . .

Allow any thoughts that might be running through your mind to drift by . . .

Trust that in about fifteen minutes you can return to the events of the day . . .

Take about ten more seconds to totally let go . . .

Now see if you can remember a day that you believe was one of the most joyful days of your life . . .

Where were you and what were you doing? . . .

Remember as many details as possible . . .

What time of year was it? . . .

Who was with you? . . .

What were you doing that made you feel joyful? . . .

What else was special about this day? . . .

Can you remember your internal dialogue? Did you say things to yourself like "This is fun" or "I love this moment" or "I enjoy being around these people"? . . .

Were there any events during that day that met your need for connection or significance or contribution? . . .

How about your need for variety or personal growth? . . .

Which needs seemed to be met the most? . . .

Think again about the highlights of that day . . .

Intensify the positive feelings you get from this memory . . .

Would you like to have more joyful days like this one? . . .

What needs to happen in your life right now in order for you to do that? . . .

Would it help if you found more ways to meet your needs? . . .

Would it help to evaluate your beliefs about an area of your life that isn't the way you want it? If so, remember to find your belief by asking, "What do I believe is important in a relationship?" or "What do I believe has to happen in order for me to feel successful?" Tailor the question to the area you want to improve . . .

In order to feel more joy, do you need to accept or release something? . . .

Do you need to forgive yourself? . . .

Do you need to forgive someone else? . . .

What would you like to do in order to release or forgive? . . .

Now feel a sense of love and peace sweeping over you, melting away any concerns that might prevent you from having the joy you desire . . .

Take a few moments to feel all your concerns being lifted from you . . .

Take a deep breath and feel the release of the old . . .

Begin to smile as you think about how your life will be full of joyful moments from now on . . .

Decide on one joyful activity you could do within the next few days that would show you that you can have more joy in your life. Maybe you could watch a funny movie, read some poetry, or spend time with children . . .

In addition, consider doing something that will bring joy into someone else's day . . .

Also think about how joyful your life would be if you dedicated time each week to just play . . .

Think about how this would enhance your life . . .

When you are ready, come back to the present time feeling cleaner and happier . . .

Become aware of your surroundings . . .

Move your body around slightly to wake it up . . .

Take a few minutes to write down any ideas that might have come.

Over the next few days pay attention to any thoughts you might have that will empower you to awaken to more joy in your life. Keep in mind the joy you would experience if you took time each week to play, laugh, and enjoy the beauty around you.

SUGGESTED READING

Awaken the Giant Within. Anthony Robbins. Fireside Books, 1992.

A New Guide to Rational Living. Albert Ellis and Robert A. Harper. Wilshire Book Company, 1975.

A Woman's Worth. Marianne Williamson. Random House, 1993.

Change Your Life and Everyone in It. Michele Weiner-Davis. Fireside Books, 1996.

Living Without Procrastination: How to Stop Postponing Your Life. Susan M. Roberts, Ph.D. New Harbinger Publications, 1995.

Spontaneous Optimism. Michael Mercer and Maryann Troiani. Castlegate Publishers, 1998.

The Pursuit of Happiness. David G. Meyers. Avon Books, 1993.
Poetic Medicine: The Healing Art of Poem Making. John Fox. Putnam, 1997.

CHAPTER TWO

The Importance
of Goals

One important step in building a life of joy is having something to look forward to. Anticipation makes us eager to awaken in the morning. We smile more often because we know something good is coming our way. When we set goals and work toward accomplishing them, our interest in life becomes heightened because we are being pulled toward a brighter tomorrow.

Great leaders throughout history all had goals. Their dreams quite often included creating something that most people viewed as impossible. Their belief in their vision kept them moving forward when others began to doubt.

For instance, two people in recent history who stayed true to their vision are South African president Nelson Mandela and Viktor Frankl. Mandela withstood twenty-five years in prison because he had a vision of equality in South Africa. And Frankl, author of *Man's Search for Meaning*, survived the horrors of Auschwitz and other Nazi concentration camps by focusing on how his life would be when he was no longer a prisoner. He consistently visualized standing in front of an audience, talking about how crucial it is that we find meaning in painful situations. His vision not only kept him alive but also empowered him to create logotherapy, a field of psychology that is now widely respected. Our goals give us not only a glimpse of a positive future but also something to focus on when facing adversity.

As children we naturally have goals. We want to make the team, have good grades, and gain parental or peer approval. As adolescents we have a strong desire to explore relationships and dream about our future. During these times we believe the world is wide open with possibility.

In adulthood, however, we tend to narrow our focus and think more in terms of financial responsibilities and family obligations. We sometimes find ourselves depressed because we have forgotten how to dream. We become skeptical about our ability to create what we want and to become the person we want to be. Too often, at the new year we make halfhearted attempts at resolutions to change that never materialize. When our desires don't come about, we shrug our shoulders and think, "I knew goal setting wouldn't work."

What's missing is sheer determination. When we have a clear

vision of what we want and commit to having it, our dreams can come true. It may take more effort than we first realized, and goals may come in different forms than we originally intended. We may also meet roadblocks along the way. None of this has to stop us. If we stay committed and push forward, we will find a way to have what we want.

Each time we complete a goal we develop more self-esteem and a greater awareness of the creative process. We may start out believing only slightly that we really have the ability to reach our goal. If we remain consistent our confidence builds and we begin to honor our dreams. Then the day comes when we look around and realize our goals have in fact come true. For a moment we forget the hard work and simply delight in the miracle of creation.

Setting Goals

Setting goals can be a magical process of self-discovery. In order to begin, we must first have a clear idea of what we want. This is fairly simple to do when we are aiming for a material object like a car, a house, or new clothes. We can read magazines, visit stores, and talk with people about their purchases in order to evaluate which items best reflect our unique style. It can be fun thinking how our lives will be enriched. We can get excited and connect with others who have similar desires.

Something begins to happen, though, when we move from strictly material goals to our deepest dreams. After we have set enough goals and made them happen, we begin to realize that we can have goals that come from a higher part of ourselves. This makes us more aware of the need to develop an overall plan for our lives that is in alignment with our greatest inspiration.

Uncovering this plan has its challenges. It takes careful consideration and trial and error to realize what we ultimately want to accomplish with our lives. We may be clear on some things, like the type of relationships we want to have, but we aren't as certain about the best career choice. Or we may be aware of our spiritual beliefs, but we haven't figured out how to incorporate them with the playful side of life.

Many times we are unaware of the direction to take because we have become accustomed to living life according to others' beliefs. All of us want to fit in and be accepted to some degree. It takes courage to listen to the small still voice inside that is guiding us toward becoming our true selves and offering our unique vision.

If we allow it, our intuition will direct us and make it easier to find our higher vision. We may have daydreams of how we would like our lives to be. We may see someone doing something and think, "I would like to do that." Or we may have a strong feeling about a particular direction in life. These are all intuitive indications of what we ought to be doing.

Another indication of what your goals should be comes from those activities that excite you or evoke your passion or natural ability. Maybe you want to buy a boat and sail around the world, write a novel, or start a business. All these desires are nudging you toward the particular path that best suits you.

You can gain greater clarity on your personal destination by asking yourself questions like "If I were living a life that brought me the most joy and purpose, what would it be like?" or "If I could live the life that I truly wanted, what would I be doing, and who would be in my life?" Honor your responses. You may see an image of the future, hear something, or get a feeling. Analyze the information that comes to you and find a way to incorporate it into your life.

Make your goals well rounded. You don't want to focus only on an ideal career and find yourself like the CEO who retired in ill health, unable to take his wife on the cruise he had been promising her for thirty years.

Include a vision for your health, your finances, your relationships, your spirituality, and your favorite activities. Carefully think through the effect your goals will have on your life. If you believe returning to school is your next step, figure out beforehand how to reconcile your finances and the needs of your family with your studies. Ask clarifying questions such as "If I did lose weight, how would my life be different?" or "How would finding a perfect partner change the way I now live?" Thinking through your goals will prevent you from working toward something and discovering it isn't what you wanted after all. It will also motivate you to honor your goals because you will get a clear picture of the positive changes they will make in your life.

Taking Action

The next step in setting goals is taking action. No matter how much we wish, hope, or dream, our goals will not manifest unless we take the necessary action to bring them about. Everything around us was created because someone first envisioned it and then worked to make it a reality. Your home was originally someone's idea that became the hard work of laborers. The lightbulbs that illuminate the dark were the vision and effort of Thomas Edison. And the telephones that we take for granted were once only a dream to Alexander Graham Bell. If these people hadn't first intuited what they wanted and then taken action, we wouldn't be enjoying our current lifestyles.

Some goals have built-in action plans. If you want to be a doctor, you know you have to go to medical school, become an intern, and choose your specialty before you can practice medicine. If you want to start your own business, you need to decide where to locate it and then come up with a financial plan.

Other goals aren't as easily mapped out. It's hard to know what's first, second, and third when it comes to meeting the right person and falling in love. And with some goals you may have a clear long-term plan but not know how to take the next step. That's why writing down your goals and reviewing them regularly can be one of the most important things you do. When you write down a goal, it deepens your commitment to making it happen. There is something about seeing it in your own handwriting that makes it more real. And regular reviews will signal your unconscious to be on the alert for new clues that can lead you forward.

When you review your goals, visualize them as being complete. Put yourself in the picture and think of the pleasure they will bring. Incorporate as many of your senses as possible. You might see yourself enjoying the goal, or you might hear yourself saying something like "I am so happy I have accomplished this." You might also hear others telling you how proud they are of you. And you might feel a sense of self-respect or jubilation.

After consistently visualizing your goals you will notice an interesting thing happening. What was once a fuzzy faraway vision becomes clear and bright. It begins to have a three-dimensional, realistic appearance. No longer is it something far out in the future; it seems tangible, as if it is already happening before your eyes.

As you keep your goals in the forefront of your mind, you become more aware of the opportunities surrounding you. You will start to notice options you once overlooked. Think about a time when you purchased something new like a car and you suddenly began noticing cars like yours everywhere. They were always there—you just didn't have a reason to notice them before. The same thing happens with your goals. You'll begin to meet people who have goals similar to yours, and for some reason you'll turn on the television just at the time a program is discussing the information you need.

Another important action step is to live as if your goals are already complete. Decide what you would be like if your dreams came true. How would you feel about life? How would you treat others? Begin to think, act, and speak this way. Our unconscious minds have a strong need to remain consistent with the way we view ourselves. And the world responds to the way we present ourselves. So create an identity that is consistent with what you want in life. This will help you prepare for your new way of living. It will also show you any hesitations or fears you might have about your goals.

Be Flexible and Consistent

If you started out with a clear goal, took action, and reviewed your goals consistently, and they still don't seem to be occurring, you may have to be flexible and shift your approach.

Often people don't succeed because either they continue to do what isn't working or they give up too soon. Those who quit prematurely will often say, "I have tried everything," when in reality they have only made three or four attempts. The people who get what they want are the ones who hang in there. They will try hundreds of ways until they finally reach a desired outcome.

I know of a woman who tried off and on for twenty years to lose excess weight. Nothing she did gave her the result she wanted. She continued to lose and regain the same fifteen pounds. Finally she shifted her focus from being thin to being healthy. By focusing on health she became aware of how food allergies and improper food combinations made her body react with excess fat. As long as she concentrated on being thin, she was unaware of the negative effect of eating certain foods. Changing her focus gave her new information that helped her meet her goal.

There is a process for creating our goals. Often we start out with enthusiasm and then become discouraged and unsure. We may work hard for a while but see few results. At times everything will seem to be coming together perfectly, and then we may go through a period where our dreams appear to be on hold. Thoughts of giving up may enter our minds. That's when we need to trust the ebb and flow of the process.

We must resist becoming too invested in achieving our goals in some preconceived way. Many paths can lead to the same destination. Some minor adjustments may be necessary. Step back and assess. Maybe your vision isn't clear enough. Or perhaps you are trying to achieve too much too quickly and need to break your goals down into smaller, more specific steps.

Sometimes it appears that things are standing still when they are actually coming together in an unseen way. The people who need to assist you may be on their way and just haven't shown up yet. Or the house you are looking for may not be on the market one week but will be the next. Relax for a while and put your list of goals in a drawer for a few days and enjoy life. This will give you the energy to refine your vision and discover the next step.

An Attitude of Gratitude

Sometimes the next step is to appreciate what we already have. When we are grateful, the abundance in our lives seems to increase. If we are focusing on what we don't have or how bad things are, we stop the flow of good. When we smile at people, they tend to smile back. And whatever we give out comes back to us multiplied.

In his book *Conversations with God* Neal Donald Walsh suggests that to manifest our desires, we offer a prayer of gratitude in advance. Thanking God beforehand builds our trust that we can have what we desire.

And remember, each experience has value no matter how inconsequential it may seem. If we are wanting more than we currently have, we can use our present situation as a stepping-stone. If someone wants to be a restaurant manager but has to start out as a busboy, he can see the merit in being where he is. He can work toward becoming a waiter and then one day the manager. If he decides through experience that the restaurant business isn't for him, he can use the skills he has learned to enhance other areas of his life.

Every step counts along the way to our goals. The menial tasks we take on are always a preparation for something better. So celebrate even the smallest accomplishments and take a moment to be grateful and to pat yourself on the back. You are actively doing what it takes to create your life the way you want it to be.

Meditation

The following meditation is designed to help you gain clarity about your goals.

Before you begin, make sure you can take fifteen minutes of

uninterrupted time to complete the meditation. Find a quiet place where you can relax.

During this meditation you will probably get several answers about your future goals. You might find it helpful to have a pen and paper handy to take notes after the meditation. Remember to read each line or paragraph and listen to your responses before moving on to the next line.

Begin the meditation by taking a couple of deep breaths. Feel your body relaxing with each breath . . .

Let your shoulders soften and release tension . . .

Shift your focus from the everyday world to the meditation . . .

Take a few more seconds to quiet your mind and relax your body . . .

Now begin to feel a sense of anticipation because you are about to uncover a new awareness of your goals . . .

Think about your current goals. What are you working toward? . . .

What about your vision of an ideal life? If you were living the life you truly wanted, what would it be like? . . .

What would you be doing? . . .

Who would be in your life? . . .

What would happen in the course of a typical day? . . .

What type of career would you have? . . .

Would you go to work each day, or would you work at home? . . .

What about your body? Would it be lean and strong? Lush or robust? . . .

Would you have the energy you need to do the things you love? . . .

Does your vision include rich relationships? . . .

Do you have a significant other? . . .

How would you relate to your family? . . .

Are there friends that you feel comfortable being around in this image? . . .

Do you enjoy your relationship with yourself? . . .

What about having time to play and enjoy the fun of life? . . .

Are there any new hobbies or adventures you would try? . . .

What would your spiritual life be like? . . .

Do you feel a connection to God and the sacredness of life? . . .

Is this a connection you would like to deepen? . . .

What about your material possessions? Would you have a new car, clothes, or jewelry that you enjoyed? Or would your home be simple but sufficient? . . .

What type of house would you live in? . . .

Where would you go on vacation? . . .

How much money would you have in the bank? . . .

Allow yourself to experience these things . . .

How grateful would you be if you were daily living this ideal? . . .

What would you say to yourself if all this were a part of your life? . . .

Move forward five yeas in your mind and imagine you have lived this lifestyle for five years . . .

Who will you have become? . . .

How will you treat others? . . .

How will they treat you? . . .

What about you would be changed? . . .

Do you have more self-confidence? . . .

Are you more loving? . . .

Can you find a way to use all that you have been blessed with to help others? . . .

Are there certain charities that you would regularly contribute to? . . .

Take a little while longer to fully live this dream . . .

In order to now have this lifestyle, what is one of the first things you need to do? . . .

Do you need to improve upon your relationships, your health, or your finances? . . .

Where would you begin? . . .

What else do you need to do? . . .

How can you now begin to act and speak as if this dream has become a reality? . . .

Will writing down these goals and reviewing them daily help you manifest this vision? . . .

What one thing can you do within the next twenty-four hours to put this dream in motion? . . .

Before we end the meditation, take another moment to experience living your ideal life . . .

When you are ready, bring your focus back to your surroundings . . .

Move your body around slightly . . .

As you become fully present, trust that as you continue to explore your goals, you will gain clarity on the specific direction to take. As your desires take on a more concrete form, you will find them becoming a part of your life.

SUGGESTED READING

A Strategy for Daily Living. Ari Kiev, M.D. The Free Press, 1973.

The 7 Habits of Highly Effective People. Stephen Covey. Fireside Books, 1989.

Unlimited Power. Anthony Robbins. Fawcett Columbine Books, 1986.

CHAPTER THREE

Prioritizing Time and Space

❧

Have you ever had one of those days when you felt that if you had to do one more thing you would be in overload? The trash is overflowing, someone is sick, the car is acting up, the bills need to be paid, and the phone won't stop ringing.

We all go through cycles where there is more to get done than we can handle. We haven't finished yesterday's obligations before we have a whole new list for today. Household duties are left undone and everything piles up. We start feeling hopeless and unsure of how to pull our lives back together. We begin to take care of what seems most urgent instead of what's most important.

The best way to prepare for hectic periods and ease the pain of feeling overwhelmed is to create a strategy for prioritizing time and organizing personal space. When there is a system in place for handling the day-to-day obligations, we can easily get our schedules back on track after dealing with one of life's emergencies. Similarly, when we've had a house full of company or a week that left little time for cleaning, we can put our surroundings back in order quickly because we have already established a place for our personal items.

This chapter is designed to help you come up with a system that works best for your individual style. Following the suggested ideas will not only help you feel more in control of your life, it will also free up some time so that you can enjoy the special moments of each day.

Gaining Control of Your Personal Time

How do we actually begin to master time management? How do we learn to balance work with play and family obligations? I believe the first step is to define exactly what is most important in our lives. In other words, to begin to consciously set real priorities. Setting priorities and sticking to them will keep us from cramming one more thing into our schedule or saying yes to being on another committee when our efforts really should stay focused on projects more important to us.

Begin to look closely at your existing responsibilities in life. Are you a parent, spouse, community leader, or office manager?

Consider each of these responsibilities. Which of them are of the highest priority? Which need more attention? Which need less?

Now take a look at your goals. Make sure you have scheduled enough time to pursue your goals as well as to handle your existing responsibilities. If one of your goals is to be healthy, then you will naturally want to set aside time to exercise, instead of waiting to see if you can fit in a workout later. And if your goal is to be a better parent, then family time must be something you protect from interruptions.

Identifying your priorities, putting them first, and then actively scheduling to stay focused on them is key. You will end up happier at the end of the day because more of the things that are important to you get done. If you worry about not having enough free time, make that one of your goals and give it priority as well. If you plan carefully, you will be surprised at the time you can find to study new subjects, watch a sunset, call a friend, or travel to exotic places.

Realize, however, that there will still be moments when a wave of sudden new responsibilities will threaten to overwhelm you. A spouse or relative may become ill and need your help, or a special project at work or school may be thrust upon you. At these moments try to stick with your basic organization; just push some responsibilities out further in the schedule. At the most difficult times you may want to ask for some help from a friend or relative. Anything you can delegate will help lighten your load.

By all means, avoid the urge to maximize your time by doing too many "on the way out the door" chores, those last-minute things we do instead of leaving on time for an appointment. We start unloading the dishwasher, watering the plants, or picking up the phone when we need to be walking out the door. Save those tasks for later. This will keep your attention where it needs to be. And it will help you arrive on time, feeling fresh and centered instead of frazzled.

Organizing Your Surroundings

The payoff from organizing your surroundings lies in the time and mental energy that can be saved and devoted to other things. All of us have our personal space organized to some degree. The question I would like to pose here is whether your organization is comprehensive enough to handle the day-to-day clutter. When we have a regular place to put things like important papers, car keys, and sunglasses, we don't waste time looking for these items or risk losing them. And as long as every belonging has a place, pickup is a breeze.

Take an inventory of your home or office and see if your personal organization needs to be fine-tuned. I would suggest three steps. First, evaluate how you currently use your space at home or in the office and decide how you might use it better. Second, buy the supplies you determine are necessary to implement a better plan. And third, make the changes. Be careful that you don't try to do too much at one time. Take a day or weekend to evaluate your surroundings, another period of time to buy supplies, and then make the changes after that. The idea is to not get overwhelmed and abandon the project. Try to see it as a fun process that will save you time and frustration in the future. Let's look at this process in more detail.

Evaluate

Go from room to room and systematically observe how you currently use your space. For example, do you tend to open the mail in one particular area of the house? Do sweaters and coats end up in the same place consistently? Does one room seem always to be cluttered with books and newspapers? Make a note of the problem areas, like a clothes closet that is so disorganized you can't find anything to wear. Or a bathroom that is full of half-empty containers of face creams and shampoos that you no longer use. Or a kitchen that is no fun to be in because the cabinets and counter space are overflowing with half-empty cartons, groceries, and kitchen gadgets.

During your evaluation, make a list of repairs that need to be made. And by all means, make a note of the items you haven't used in a long time. Decide what can be thrown away, recycled, donated, or sold at a garage sale. The goal is to eliminate as much clutter as possible.

Once you've taken an inventory, you are ready to decide how to best use your space. Begin with one room or particular problem area within the room and think about how it would be if used optimally. For example, if you have a laundry room that is in disarray, decide how you want the room to look and function once it is organized. Maybe items have gravitated in there because it is a natural stopping point or there is no other place to put certain things that come into your home. Or maybe the mess is created by laundry baskets full of clean clothes that aren't put away once they come out of the dryer. Decide what should stay and what should go. If there are nonclothing items in the room, can you find a better place for them, or do you want to put up shelves to hold them? If the clutter is clothing, you might consider clothes bins and shelves.

Another example might be a corner of a room where newspapers pile up. You might determine it is still the best spot to read the paper, since your reading chair is there, but adding a basket or end table would help keep the space neater. You might also find it helpful to have a recycling bin nearby to store the papers once they have been read.

If you find that you get stuck trying to figure out the best layout for your home or office, flip through magazines and organiz-

ing catalogs for ideas. You may want to hire a professional organizer. Look through your phone book for a local person. Or
write or call the National Association of Professional Organizers
for a referral to organizers in your area. Their address is 1033 La
Posada Drive, Suite 220, Austin, TX 78752 (512-206-0151).
Their Web address is *www.napo.net.*

The idea behind organizing your space is to make yourself
more comfortable and your desired lifestyle more achievable.
Instead of forcing yourself to become more disciplined about
having a pristine environment, find a system that suits you. If
folding a hand towel and neatly placing it on a towel bar after
each use is too time-consuming for you or your family, buy
towel hooks instead. This way, everyone will be more likely to
return the towels. And if the mail and school papers end up in
one room, don't expect them to magically migrate to your desk.
Follow the flow of the house and put a collection bin, trash can,
or desk in that room.

If you live with others who don't share your need for organization, determine their patterns and work within their parameters. If they always leave books, magazines, and receipts in
certain areas, decide how to house those items. To some degree
the other people you live with will have to agree to organizational changes in common areas. If they balk, then start with
your personal space and office. Usually, once they see how
much time you save, they'll become interested.

Purchase What You Need

After you have surveyed your home and office and have improvements in mind, the second step you need to take is to make a list of necessary supplies. Remember to include lightbulbs, cleaning supplies, trash bags, and tools for repairs.

Now's the time to go shopping or to place a catalog order. Remember, don't scrimp. Items that will save you time and mental anguish are well worth the money.

Take Action

The third step, when you are ready, is to set aside several hours to put your organizational system in place. Begin in an area where you will see results the fastest. This will motivate you to organize the rest of your home or office. Work on only one area at a time. Often we abandon a project in the middle because we didn't break it down into manageable segments. Maybe you have decided to organize your bedroom, and your clothes closet is your biggest concern. Begin with the closet and complete its organization before moving to other parts of the room.

Let's use organizing your clothes closet as an example. Begin by sorting through your clothes. You may find it helpful to follow the advice of Julie Morgenstern, author of *Organizing from the Inside Out.* She suggests having three boxes handy, one box labeled "give away," another labeled "belongs elsewhere," and a third labeled "needs repair." Using this system will help you make quick decisions about the articles you come across. If it isn't something you need, use frequently, or enjoy wearing, get rid of it. It is just taking up space. If you find some articles you can't part with because you think you might one day wear them, at least get them out of your closet and into more permanent storage so you will be able to find the things you do wear regularly.

Once you know what you are going to keep, begin putting everything in order. Maybe you want to have all the shirts in one place and all the pants in another. You may want to break your system down further and organize by color and season. Arrange the clothes and shoes you use the most often so that they are the easiest to get to and return.

During this active phase of organizing your surroundings, you might want to consider other structural changes. For instance, you might need to rearrange where you think the current layout hampers your family's daily traffic flow. By simply moving a lamp or table a few feet you may open up easy access from one room to the next. A picture that seems flat or dull in one room may brighten and complete another room. Find the right home for every item in your space.

For more tips on how to arrange your home or office, consider researching *feng shui*, the ancient art of placement. The

Chinese are most noted for this principle of consciously placing objects around or within a building. They believe strategic placement ensures health and prosperity. The reading list at the end of this chapter includes books on this subject.

Once your new organizational system is in place, spend a few weeks consciously using the system. Be committed to forming new habits. Then review what you have done to see if everything is actually working better and saving time. If you still find that some rooms are too cluttered, rethink that space. Ideally your system will enable you to keep your surroundings in order with minimum care.

Michelle's Story

A good example of how our lives can change when we organize our time and space is demonstrated by the experience of a young woman named Michelle. When she was a freshman in college, Michelle began to feel her life was out of control. Her college courses were much more difficult than she was prepared for. And since she was away from home for the first time, she didn't know how to manage her time. Instead of studying, she used her new freedom to play.

A few months into the first semester, Michelle began to feel crowded in a small apartment with two messy roommates who wanted to party all the time. Their constant presence made it impossible for her to find enough personal space.

When things got bad enough, Michelle confided in her parents. They encouraged her to go to a school counselor, who helped Michelle realize how her behavior was perpetuating a sense of helplessness. The counselor recommended that Michelle first straighten up her apartment and car so that she could gain an immediate sense of control. Then the counselor helped her create a schedule that included studying and spending time with friends.

Michelle left the counselor's office and immediately began cleaning and organizing. She spent a weekend alone at a friend's house and mapped out a plan for getting her life back on track. She returned to her apartment with a new commitment to organizing her surroundings and budgeting her time.

Within a few weeks Michelle began to feel like her old productive self. She encouraged her roommates to become neater by posting a cleaning schedule. And she negotiated an hour a day of alone time for herself in the apartment when her roommates were in class, at the library, or with friends. Michelle also learned to take her role as a student more seriously by staying committed to her study schedule.

These behavior changes lasted beyond college. When she married and began having children, Michelle continued to schedule time for herself. She knew that in order to be a good wife and mother, she had to have a few hours here and there to be alone and think. She also developed an organizational system that met her family's lifestyle.

Michelle's story is a reminder of the necessity of a good organizational system. Once we find the system that works best for us, we can incorporate it into every phase of our lives.

Meditation

This meditation is designed to help you feel more in control of your life by organizing your surroundings and managing your time. It is somewhat different from the others in the book. While reading through it, you might want to drift in and out of visualizing what's mentioned and taking notes as they come to you. Or you can treat it the way you would any of the other meditations and read through it before writing anything down. Experiment and see which format is most helpful to you.

This meditative exercise will take you about fifteen minutes to complete. As you read, remember to focus on one line or paragraph at a time. When you have fulfilled the request of each line or paragraph, move on to the next line.

Before you begin, make sure you are in a quiet, comfortable place where you can spend uninterrupted time alone.

Begin the meditation by lowering your shoulders and relaxing your neck and back . . .

Move your body around a little to help it relax even more . . .

Take a deep breath and feel yourself letting go . . .

Trust that this is the most important thing you could be doing right now . . .

Let all other thoughts drift by . . .

Take about fifteen more seconds to relax and quiet your mind . . .

Let's focus first on time management.

Think about the way you regularly use your time. What do you normally accomplish in a day? . . .

What do you accomplish in a week? . . .

What seems to work well with the way you currently schedule your time? . . .

Do you have certain routines that work well for you? Maybe you have a specific day you go to the market, and another day when you go out to dinner with your friends or spouse . . .

What doesn't seem to work well with the way you use your time? . . .

Do you feel you are always rushing? . . .

Are you unable to accomplish as much as you would like? . . .

Do you have enough quality time with your family and friends? . . .

What is it you would like to do that you can't seem to find time for? . . .

How would you ideally like to spend your time? . . .

What would you eliminate from your current schedule if you could? . . .

What would you add? . . .

What needs to happen in order for you to use your time the way you want to? . . .

Would it help you to clarify what's most important to you in life and then schedule your days around your priorities? . . .

Are there obligations you could delegate? . . .

Would you need to put certain projects on hold for now? . . .

Is there anything you could do today that would help you use your time more efficiently? . . .

What else could you do? . . .

Before we move on to organizing your surroundings, see if any more ideas come to you about how to change the way you use your time . . .

Let's focus now on organizing your surroundings to help you save time.

Think about one room in your home that you are eager to put in order . . .

What about the way the room is currently organized works well for you? . . .

What doesn't work well? Is it hard to clean because there is too much clutter? Are you embarrassed by the mess? . . .

Do you find that the disorganization of this room preoccupies your mind sometimes? . . .

What seems to be creating the problem: not enough storage space, papers piling up, or family members leaving things lying around? . . .

How do you want to use this space? What actually belongs in here? . . .

If you could use this room exactly the way you wanted to, how would you do it? . . .

What would you eliminate or install first? . . .

What other changes would you make? . . .

See this room being the way you want it to be and think of how it would be to spend time here once it is organized . . .

If this room were organized the way you wanted, how would it improve your lifestyle? Would you feel more comfortable when you had visitors, would it end family friction, or would it help you feel better about yourself? . . .

If this room did become messy because of a busy week, would you be able to put it back in order quickly? . . .

If you decide to organize this room in the near future, where would you begin? . . .

Will you need someone to help you? . . .

Are there items you need to buy? . . .

What else do you need to do? . . .

How soon would you like to start organizing? . . .

Take a few minutes to think of anything else you need to do to help you implement your new system . . .

Return to your vision of how this room will be once it is organized and enjoy being there a little longer . . .

When you are ready to end the meditation, bring your focus back to present time . . .

Move your body around slightly and ground yourself by focusing first on your feet and then on your neck and shoulders . . .

Before you return to the day, make sure to write down your ideas and to schedule the time to begin your organization.

Keep the questions asked in this meditation in mind when you are thinking about organizing your office. Just substitute the word "office" for the word "room."

SUGGESTED READING

Feng Shui: The Chinese Art of Placement. Sarah Rossbach. E.P. Dutton, 1995.

Interior Design with Feng Shui. Sarah Rossbach. Penguin Books, 1987.

The Chinese Art of Designing a Harmonious Environment. Derek Walters. Simon & Schuster, 1989.

First Things First. Stephen R. Covey. Fireside Books, 1995.

Organizing from the Inside Out. Julie Morgenstern. Owl Books, 1998.

Taming the Paper Tiger at Home. Barbara Hemphill. Kiplinger Books, 1998.

Taming the Paper Tiger at Work. Barbara Hemphill. Kiplinger Books, 1998.

Working Mothers 101. Katherine Wyse Goldman. HarperPerennial, 1998.

The Western Guide to Feng Shui: Creating Balance, Harmony, and Prosperity in Your Environment. Terah Kathryn Collins. Hay House, 1996.

CHAPTER FOUR

Effective Communication

❧

Throughout our lives each of us comes into contact with thousands of people. With some of them we feel an instant rapport. Conversation seems effortless and uplifting, giving us the sense that the connection transcends words. We know what the other person is going to say before he says it. In the case of old friends we often feel as though time itself doesn't matter, that we can be separated for months or years and our sense of closeness seems to pick up where it ended.

We also encounter the opposite situation. We find ourselves struggling to communicate with people with whom we feel totally out of sync. Despite our best efforts, conversations are difficult and superficial. Not only do we have trouble understanding the concepts they are trying to relate, their entire point of view seems foreign. And from all that we can tell, our own ideas appear equally unintelligible to them.

These difficult interactions can throw us off balance and affect our sense of joy. What are we to do in such situations, especially if these difficulties arise with people who are important to us, such as family members, coworkers, and employers?

Some relationships will always be difficult, but I believe that most can be improved significantly by applying some basic guidelines. In most cases the conflict is a result of differing beliefs about life instead of an inherent incompatibility. Our challenge is to bridge these barriers of thought, to reach across differing backgrounds and definitions so we can understand each other. The first step in this process is listening.

Listening

Most experts in communication emphasize the power of attentive listening. Too often in conversation we focus not on what the other person is saying, but on what we are going to say in response. At times we cut the other person off even before she has finished making her point.

To resolve difficult interactions, we have to go beyond a superficial attempt at understanding. We have to listen deeply for the clues that show us a meaning beneath the words. If we listen to someone carefully, we will hear certain words or phrases that describe how the other person views the world. What's more, when we listen deeply to others, it makes them feel validated and understood. It lifts them into a higher awareness of who they are and what they believe. This is similar to what happens in the active listening of a therapeutic situation.

Poet John Fox understands the power of being heard. He addresses this idea in his poem "When Someone Deeply Listens to You." He writes:

i

When someone deeply listens to you
it is like holding out a dented cup
you've had since childhood
and watching it fill up with
cold, fresh water.
When it balances on top of the brim,
you are understood.
When it overflows and touches your skin,
you are loved.

ii

When someone deeply listens to you,
the room where you stay
starts a new life

and the place where you wrote
your first poem
begins to glow in your mind's eye.
It is as if gold has been discovered!

iii

When someone deeply listens to you,
your barefeet are on the earth
and a beloved land that seemed distant
is now at home within you.

Listening is the key to good communication. It puts you in a position to fully explore the inner world of the person you are interacting with.

Different Points of View

Even though we tend to assume we are much like everyone else in our culture, each of us has his own beliefs and assumptions about the nature of life. These assumptions are formed through years of experience, beginning in childhood and continuing throughout our entire lives. Each experience adds to our unique value system and point of view. For instance, a person who grew up with a loving, stable family would view the world differently than a person who spent his childhood in and out of foster homes. Similarly, a person who has undergone years of stress created by a chronic disease will have a different appreciation for life than a person who has never been ill.

Our differences can sometimes be startling when they show up. Have you ever had the experience of talking with someone, assuming you are being understood, when suddenly you realize the other person has no idea of what you just said? Or the person becomes upset for seemingly no reason? Chances are, something you said didn't make sense within this person's experience. Or perhaps your words came across as a put-down and created a defensive reaction.

There is a good probability that the breakdown in communication happened because the other person assigned a different meaning than you intended to a word or phrase you used. This is more common than many of us think.

To clarify this point, think about an ordinary word like "wealth." It can conjure up a thousand connotations. To one person "wealth" may mean being able to pay bills on time and having enough money left over to take the family to dinner and a movie once a month. To someone else "wealth" will mean owning three homes and a private jet. And to yet another person "wealth" may mean having a healthy family and loving friends. Our unique definitions are all very subjective, sensitive, and sometimes unconscious.

Nowhere else are our differences more apparent than during

male-female interactions. In his book *Men Are from Mars, Women Are from Venus,* John Gray brings attention to the fact that men and women have different perspectives about relationships and life. These differences often lead to heated debates, especially when it comes to parenting, managing money, or even how to stay connected romantically. A woman may believe that in order to be connected and loving, she and her partner must spend time together intimately talking. A man may believe that connection and love come from just being together. After a night of watching television the woman might say, "We never do anything together." The man would be bewildered by this statement. In his model of the world they have been doing something together the entire evening. His response might be, "How can you say that? We've been together all night."

If they aren't careful, the conversation could quickly become argumentative and defensive. The man might think, "Nothing I do makes her happy." And the woman would think, "He just doesn't understand." The different perspectives come solely from differing definitions about what it means to "be together."

To heal the conflict, it would help the couple to recognize they have different assumptions of what it means to be intimate. If the man had listened more closely, and gained more information on what the woman meant by her statement, he would have been less confused about the woman's complaint and more understanding of her needs. She may actually be saying, "I need some quiet, uninterrupted time with you to talk about what's happening in our lives and how we feel about each other." Similarly, if the woman was attuned to the man's definition of what "together" meant, she could begin to understand why they didn't spend a lot of time talking.

Situations like these are not uncommon. We may hear a statement or request from another person and think, "This person is stupid or wrong." What's actually happening is that the other person is sharing his beliefs, based on his experiences. If we disagree with what seems perfectly logical to him, we will shut down communication immediately.

If we find ourselves becoming defensive, it helps to ask the other person to define what he meant by his statement. We may realize we misinterpreted his meaning altogether. And if we are the ones who say something that is misunderstood, it helps to make statements like "Perhaps I wasn't very clear with my point" or "Let me say that another way." This will disarm the other person and give him the opportunity to explain what he thought was said.

Also make sure that you are being understood by asking, "Do you know what I mean?" or "Did that make sense?" When you are trying to convey an important point, you may find it helpful to have your listener repeat what you said. This way you can determine what he actually heard.

Check body language. By noticing a look on someone's face or maybe the tilt of a head, you will be able to tell if you were understood or if your statements were unclear.

Control Dramas

There will be times when we feel not just misunderstood or confused in an interaction but somehow manipulated or subtly put down. As we try to make sense out of what is happening, we might realize we are being placed in a predetermined role, pulled into a drama of some kind created by this other person. The famed interaction psychologist Eric Berne called these manipulations the "games people play."

My husband, James Redfield, has related these games to spirituality in his book *The Celestine Prophecy* by calling them "control dramas." Control dramas are repeated scripts we all tend to play when we become fearful in order to win attention and feel better about ourselves. He describes these behaviors as falling into one of four types: the Poor Me, the Aloof, the Interrogator, and the Intimidator.

Those who are interested in maintaining a joyful life must come to grips with these often unconscious games and learn to weave their way through such interaction without a loss of energy or self-respect. With patience, practice, and understanding, it can be done. Becoming familiar with these four control dramas will further your ability to deal with the ego battles they create. Keep in mind they are acted out because of fear and insecurity.

Let's begin by talking about the Poor Me drama. It is the most passive behavior of the four. Poor Me sees the world as basically unsafe and harmful and always expects that dreadful events, outside his control, are coming around every corner to impact his life. From a Poor Me's point of view, his only hope is that someone will rescue him. The irony is he doesn't believe anyone will help, so he relies on cajoling and guilt-tripping to get what he wants. When someone defers to him, he feels safe.

Usually this behavior stems from abusive or overly critical parents who gave the Poor Me the idea he was powerless. As a child the Poor Me's only success came when he could induce sympathy in others.

When you find yourself in a conversation or relationship with a person who is acting out a Poor Me script, it helps to stay centered in your own viewpoint. By understanding that you are not responsible for the other person's happiness, you will find yourself more willing to help him. Also helpful is projecting positive regard and energy toward the individual. Realize this control drama was created in the first place because the individual has a sense of anxiety and powerlessness. Giving him love, instead of buying into a guilt trip, allows him to feel as comfortable as possible.

The next step can be a touchy one. When it seems right, find a way to tell him how you feel in his presence. In other words, describe the drama you feel you are being pulled into. Be prepared to give examples of times in the past when you felt manipulated. As you probably know, it is not easy to hear criticism from others, so realize he may not easily accept what you have to say. Here it is important to show your love and a willingness to stay in the relationship, if it can move past the game.

You might find it helpful to imagine talking with this person before you have an actual conversation. Or you could role-play with a friend. See the conversation going in a positive way.

Also allow yourself or the other person to break off the relationship for a while if that is what seems best. You can continue to love him from a distance and see him being happy and healthy.

What if you realize that you yourself sometimes act out a Poor Me control drama? It might be a little uncomfortable to realize at first, but becoming aware is a great first step in healing. Work to stay conscious of the fact that you sometimes try to make people feel guilty. And remember how bad it can feel when someone tries to manipulate you. Most people avoid others who make them feel bad about themselves, even if it is a family member.

When you find yourself saying something that sounds guilt-inducing, like "Why don't you ever call me?" think about the effect it might have on someone. Consider what you could do in the moment to make yourself feel better. Get clear on what you might be afraid of. And determine which of your human needs may not be getting met.

Also consider that when you are loving and supportive to

others, people go out of their way to have contact with you. If you think it might help you break your patterns, work with a counselor for a while. A therapist might be able to help you develop more self-love and come up with a plan of action that can help you change your Poor Me patterns.

The Aloof script is another control drama you might encounter. It is slightly more aggressive than the Poor Me. In this drama the person views the world as a place filled with criticism and condemnation and so tends to be very vague about the details of what's happening in her life. You may ask an Aloof how her day was, and typically she will make unrevealing statements such as "It was fine" or "Not much occurred."

Aloofs don't feel they can trust others with their personal information. As children they had people in their lives who pried into their personal business and used it against them, either by making fun of them or by criticizing them. As adults they withhold information out of fear and use their vagueness to feel safe during interactions. After all, when we are confused about who a person is, we tend to focus our attention on her by asking questions that will help us understand her. When we do this, we are deferring to the Aloof's view of things, at least for a while. However, when the process of trying to gain information goes on too long, we realize we are being manipulated.

When dealing with someone who is playing out an Aloof script, realize that they are actually saying, "I am afraid you are going to criticize me like people in the past." Build as much trust as possible with this person. Find out her model of a trust-worthy person. Be patient when she moves away and realize she will come back around. As with the Poor Me, give her the energy she needs without buying into the drama. And again, in these situations, when it's right, we must name the game.

Tell her that when you are with her, you feel as if you can't get a straight answer to simple questions. And that it seems as though she is being distant in order to manipulate attention without being truly present in the relationship.

If you find yourself acting Aloof at times, decide what your motivation really is. Do you have reason to be guarded, or is it merely a habit to keep people mystified? Do you like the attention it gets you? Some people you encounter shouldn't be trusted. They haven't developed the maturity of a trustworthy person. Yet many people have. And if you are manipulating someone who really cares about you, consider how this behavior wears people out. They will eventually give up the chase, even the ones who love you.

A third control drama, one that is even more aggressive, is the Interrogator. In this drama a person views the world as disordered and chaotic and thus unsafe. Such a drama is typically produced in a family where the person felt neglected and unparented. In this type of environment the person began to feel as though he was responsible for keeping the family together and learned to gain attention by correcting the faults of others.

He typically ends up in relationships with people who are distant and aloof.

When we enter a conversation with someone who is playing out this drama, we immediately begin to feel as though our competency is in question. If we share information about ourselves, we may hear a response such as "I can't believe you said that" or "That was not a smart thing to do." If we are caught up in the drama, we will instantly begin to pick our words carefully and restrict our behavior. This way we defer to the Interrogator's role, which gives him the attention he desires.

Again, in order to stay out of this unconscious drama, you must first project positive energy and respect to the person. Let him know he is special. But when you can make him aware that you feel criticized when you are around him, don't argue about whether his criticisms are valid. That will only sidetrack the issue. Keep the conversation on the fact that you feel criticized. When you tell a person this with as much regard for him as possible, the game will end and the conversation and relationship can move into authentic sharing of information.

As with the other control dramas, if you find yourself acting out an Interrogator script, you need to begin to monitor yourself. Become aware of how often you criticize other people, as well as yourself. You may find yourself flipping back and forth from feeling you are better than others to feeling you are less than others.

Maybe you have become an expert in thinking ahead and

avoiding trouble in order to handle life situations. But there are better ways to intervene in someone's life than being pedantic. If you believe someone is about to make a mistake, think of a similar situation that happened to you and talk about how you handled it or wished that you had handled it. This will keep you from placing yourself in a position of authority. If you find yourself being critical of another person, consider doing what a friend of mine does. If she says something she regrets, she will stop midsentence and say, "I didn't like what I just said. And if it didn't feel good to me, then I know it didn't feel good to you. I am going to back up and say something else." This simple courtesy will help heal even the worst comments.

The last of the four control dramas and the most aggressive is the Intimidator. In this script a person repeats a childhood situation in which she was abused and left in a chaotic environment without guidance. In this atmosphere she learned to take her punishment only so long and then lashed out violently toward siblings or other peers. As an adult the attitude of "not taking it anymore" creates a repeated drama where she walks around acting as if she might go out of control at any moment. This makes everyone around her watch closely out of fear, giving her the attention she needs in order to feel secure inside.

Dealing with an Intimidator can be tricky at times. When you find yourself interacting or in a relationship with someone who tends to explode, it is important to focus on safety first. Certainly you want to tell her how she makes you feel, but often this can only be done from a safe distance. This is especially important if the Intimidator is a close friend or a spouse. Also be prepared for this person to switch into a Poor Me role and make pleas of "Don't leave me, I'll never do it again." At this point you will have to decide if she is being sincere or just saying that out of fear. She may be ready to change. But realistically, remember that most people won't change until things get bad enough. And you don't necessarily need to be around when it gets to that point.

If you realize that you use the Intimidator script, find someone who can help you analyze this tendency. Often the solution is to learn to nurture yourself and others. Come up with another way to handle your anger. Practice by visualizing a situation where you are typically fearful and angry and then see yourself being able to calmly express your feelings openly and honestly. Take responsibility for the situation. Realize that the old behavior is a drama left over from the past and that everyone is not out to hurt you or fight with you.

If you tend to react more negatively to one person than others, consistently visualize being around this person without playing the same old game. Work to get to a place where you feel a sense of inner peace and stability when around others.

In regard to all these dramas, I want to remind you that they are merely unconscious strategies that we use to force others to defer to us—to give us attention and the sense of importance that comes from being the focus of their energy. But it is a false sense of peace and it never lasts. Most people are doing the best they can to survive and deal with their own issues. It doesn't benefit anyone when we try to get our sense of self-esteem from them.

To stay in a greater state of joy, we must find our own energy inside. We don't have to win with others. We can stay centered and be the one who takes responsibility and brings the relationship back to authenticity.

In order to do this, you must take a higher stance. This will require not only compassion but also emotional maturity. It is not easy to stay in a loving place when someone is playing a game, unless we have done enough inner work to understand that the person is relating from a place of pain and fear.

As Plato said, "The unexamined life is not worth living." Take time to examine your behaviors and reactions to others. When you lead from a place of inner strength and peace, you become a truly effective communicator that people not only respect but also want to connect with.

Meditation

This meditation is designed to help you become a more effective communicator.

During the meditation you will be led through a mental exercise where you choose a person that you have had difficulty communicating with in the past and examine what might have gone wrong. Then you will be encouraged to make changes that will increase the probability of a smoother future interaction with this person.

As you read through the meditation, focus on each line or paragraph before continuing on.

Prepare for the meditation by finding a quiet spot where you can be uninterrupted for about fifteen minutes.

Begin the meditation by getting comfortable . . .

Move your body around slightly to help it relax . . .

Let any outside concerns melt away . . .

Remember that you can return to the events of the day in about fifteen minutes . . .

Take a few deep breaths to help your body let go even more . . .

Take about ten more seconds to prepare . . .

Now imagine that it is a beautiful spring day and you are somewhere in nature . . .

Where are you—in the park, in the country, or in a flower garden? . . .

What do your surroundings look like? . . .

Find a spot to rest . . .

Take a moment to listen to the sounds and smell the freshness of the air . . .

While enjoying the beauty around you, begin to think about whether or not you consider yourself a good listener . . .

Do you usually allow people to finish their sentences? . . .

Can you listen closely enough to elicit someone's model of the world? . . .

Can you think of a time in your life when you really listened to someone? . . .

Could you tell how much he or she appreciated being heard? . . .

Was there ever a time when you felt someone was deeply listening to you? . . .

Did having this person listen to you influence your ability to open up and communicate? . . .

Did you or the person you were talking with begin to get new ideas and understandings? . . .

Think about the people in your life with whom you seem to communicate well . . .

What makes the communication effortless? . . .

Now think about a person who is currently in your life with whom you have difficult conversations. Choose someone with whom you are interested in improving communication . . .

How can you tell that your conversations don't flow well? . . .

Do you think the two of you misunderstand each other because of differing beliefs about life or the way something should be done? . . .

Do you think your points of view come from dramatically different backgrounds or likes and dislikes? . . .

How do you feel when you are around this person? . . .

What is your body language when the two of you are together? . . .

What about your tone of voice? . . .

Do the two of you tend to act out control dramas when you come together? . . .

If so, is the other person more of a Poor Me, an Aloof, an Interrogator, or an Intimidator? . . .

What about you? . . .

What would help the two of you understand each other better? . . .

Would it help the conversation if you shifted your body language? . . .

What about your tone of voice? Could it be more calm and even when you are speaking with this person? . . .

What about listening? Would it help if this person felt heard? . . .

Would it help if he or she listened to you? . . .

Can you find a way to respect this person's point of view? . . .

Could you use some of this person's key words or phrases when you're speaking to him or her to create a better rapport? . . .

What else would help the conversation? . . .

Imagine that for a change you had an interaction with this person that went well. How would that appear? . . .

If at any point during the conversation you feel you want to act out an old pattern, how could you interrupt that script? . . .

Would it help you to breathe or to listen more carefully or to count to ten before you say anything? . . .

Would it help to ask questions to clarify what this person is saying? . . .

Create a good image or feeling of you breaking your pattern and the conversation flowing smoothly . . .

Continue to experience the conversation going well . . .

How would you feel if you were able to have this type of positive interaction with this person? . . .

How would it affect your life? . . .

Before we end the meditation, spend more time thinking about a future conversation with this person going well . . .

When you are ready to come out of the meditation, bring this image back with you to present time . . .

Move your body around to gently wake it up . . .

Stretch slightly . . .

And become aware of your surroundings.

Over the next few weeks focus on improving your difficult interactions. Get a clear image of how conversations could flow better. And find a way to break your old reactionary patterns.

Continue to concentrate on one person at a time. Once you feel you are able to communicate in an effective way with the person you have chosen, test your ability. If it doesn't go as well as planned, practice again. As long as you sincerely want to improve your communications with this person, you will eventually reach a level of interaction that is comfortable.

SUGGESTED READING

Divorce Busting. Michele Weiner-Davis. Fireside Books, 1993.

Don't Shoot the Dog. Karen Pryor. Bantam Books, 1984.

Men Are from Mars, Women are from Venus. John Gray. Harper-Collins, 1992.

The Celestine Prophecy. James Redfield. Warner Books, 1994.

The Celestine Vision. James Redfield. Warner Books, 1997.

CHAPTER FIVE

Finding Inner Peace

❧

O f all the elements of creating a life of joy, achieving a state of inner peace is most important. We find a feeling of inner peace when we have a sense of mental control and clarity along with an understanding of how we are part of a bigger plan in life.

Although you may not feel like it at times, each of us has the ability to develop a sense of peace. Some people find it through traditional religions and in times of prayer and meditation. Others discover it while engaging in an outdoor activity such as golf, skiing, or hiking. Still others find it through the discipline of tai chi or dance or art.

Whatever the means, we can enhance our sense of joy in life by finding an experience that helps quiet our minds while it teaches us that we are part of a greater design. Once we have this experience, we will want to maintain the inner peace it brings. But sustaining that sense of inner peace is often the most difficult part. It is one thing to have a sense of the peace when we are alone or in the calm beauty of nature. It is something else to hold on to this state when we are confronted with the challenges of normal day-to-day living. Yet I believe there are methods and habits we can acquire that will help us maintain this state of tranquillity, alert us when we lose it, and help us regain it.

Internal Dialogue

In the course of a day thousands of thoughts enter our minds. We think about work, the people we love, what to eat, which movie to see. We also worry about people or situations. Too many of these concerns can occupy our time, preventing us from feeling a sense of joy and inner peace in the moment.

One way to calm our concerns is to monitor and change our internal dialogue. What we say to ourselves has a profound effect on our sense of peace, even more so than what others say to us. Just ask any top-performing athlete or company executive, and they will tell you that their success in life has a connection to the way they think and speak to themselves.

If we keep our primary thoughts on what has gone wrong or what could go wrong, we begin to lose hope and even speak to ourselves in doubtful ways. Our internal dialogue can disintegrate into statements like "I'll never be able to handle this situation" or "I don't know what to do" or, worse, "I don't think anything can help this problem." Statements like these leave us with a sense of defeat and avoidance and set us up to keep repeating the same frustrating patterns in our lives.

Shifting our internal conversations will create a change in our behavior. When we begin to speak to ourselves in encouraging ways, something magical happens. We begin to feel better about ourselves, which gives us the energy to pursue our goals and try new things. We become more self-forgiving when we make mistakes, and more gentle with others.

Changing our internal dialogue takes practice, but it can be done by following a few simple guidelines. The first step is to recognize your personal pattern of self-talk. Once you watch yourself closely for a while, you may be astounded at what you find. Most of us would never allow someone to speak to us in a cruel or demeaning way, yet we think nothing of unleashing a torrent of criticism toward our own behavior during times of fear and doubt.

Spend time noticing how you talk to yourself. You might even want to keep a journal. Pay attention to the way you greet the day and how you describe events that take place. Listen to the words you say when you make a mistake. Does your response tend to be, "That was so stupid, I can't believe I did that"? Or do you say, "Oh well, I guess the best thing to do is learn what I can from this"?

Equally important is noticing the way you identify yourself. Maybe you think of yourself as not being a good organizer. You say to yourself, "I am not a good organizer. My father wasn't a good organizer and neither was my grandfather." Consider how a label like this will affect your enthusiasm and goal setting. Maybe you don't plan well now, but as long as you identify yourself in that way, you won't feel encouraged to improve. You won't even notice when you do organize your time well.

The next step is to begin to change your negative dialogue every time you become aware of it. Whenever you realize you are becoming self-critical, shift the words immediately to a positive expression. Admit your mistakes and find ways to encourage self-improvement. Lighten up and become your biggest fan. Each time you change your dialogue you will find your self-esteem increasing. And you will be more willing to make a second attempt in an area you didn't get right the first time.

It is also very important to change the way you describe your conversations with others. Let's say you just had a difficult interaction with a coworker or relative. If you find yourself saying, "That person violated me," you are going to encourage negative feelings. If you say to yourself instead, "Something must be bothering that person for him to speak that way to me," you might calm yourself down.

Once again a shift in internal dialogue can change the way you view the situation. As long as we embellish the painful side of a personal interaction, we will feel like a victim who is powerless to do anything about what has happened. If we instead consider that the other person was just having a bad day, and his rude behavior wasn't about us, we might discover our own capacity for compassion and understanding.

How to Stop Worrying

Another way we can maintain our inner peace is to stop worrying about situations we can't change or control. We wish we could change the past; we wish we could change behavior in others; we wish we could change the weather. Even when we face a situation that is impossible to change, we often keep trying or worry about it obsessively.

One way to begin to break this habit is to write down the concerns running through your mind and then look over the list to decide what can be changed and what can't. Our goal should be to take action when possible and find a way to release the rest.

Most of us also tend to worry about future events. We might be concerned about whether or not the new people we meet will like us, whether we are going to fail an upcoming exam, or whether we might lose the people we love and not be able to handle the pain. Many times we scare ourselves by thinking about what could go wrong instead of visualizing situations turning out the way we want. What's interesting is that most often things aren't as bad as we fear. Think of the times in your life when you worried constantly about something and then found that when the event occurred, it was far less frightening than you imagined. Or you handled the situation much better than you thought you could.

Another area of worry is being too concerned about other people's problems. Most of us worry about the people we love because we don't want to see them get hurt. We sometimes go out of our way to help them even when they don't want to help themselves. This can drain us of our time and energy if we aren't careful. As is the case with all of us, the people we love are ultimately responsible for themselves, and if we become too controlling or sheltering of others, they can be denied important opportunities to care for themselves that will strengthen them to face life's challenges.

This is not to say that we can't find a way to teach, coach, and mentor others. But if we become overly protective and always rescue those we care about, they won't move through their own difficulties and develop the self-esteem and confidence they need.

Worrying too much about others can even injure our health. Let me explain what I mean. A friend of mine told me about a man she met at a weekend conference for a small group of therapists. The man's name was Paul, and he had learned the hard way about the high cost of worrying too much about others.

My friend said Paul was a wonderful addition to the conference. He participated fully during the group exercises and often made comments that sparked new awareness. One thing my friend noticed was that Paul consistently went off on his own during the meal breaks instead of eating with the group. This surprised her, since Paul had always been eager to connect with others during the conference meetings.

During dinner she saw Paul sitting on a bench in the park across the street and decided to walk over and strike up a conversation. She politely asked why he never joined the group at mealtimes. Paul said that spending time alone to read or think about what he had learned during the conference kept him from becoming too enmeshed with other people and their problems. He told my friend of how in the past he had tried to care for every person he met, and how that behavior became draining. Because he was sensitive to the pain of others, he would listen to their problems and then offer advice. Often the people he attracted would complain about their situation instead of taking steps to change it. Paul would become frustrated and sometimes controlling. He really wanted others to be happy, and he felt he knew best.

He explained to my friend how his behavior shifted rapidly when he was diagnosed with a life-threatening illness and given only months to live. Realizing he had limited amounts of time and energy, Paul began to focus on getting well instead of taking care of others. He noticed that as long as he was caring for himself, others seemed to take better care of themselves. His friends and family members stopped expecting him to solve their problems.

Occasionally he would see people he loved going through painful situations as a result of their decisions, but he no longer felt responsible for their happiness. He learned to turn their problems over to a higher power and trust they would be cared for in a way that supported their highest good. As a consequence, he began to lighten up and have more fun. He also beat his illness.

Paul's experience helped him make the decision to be around people in situations that felt healthy. Whenever he found himself being too concerned about someone, he would remember to set his own personal boundaries and honor the boundaries of others.

Like Paul, we all have to find a way to stop being too controlling and to stop worrying in general. One way to let situations go that we can't control is to take Paul's advice and turn them over to a higher power. This can be done by saying a prayer similar to the Serenity Prayer that has been adopted by Alcoholics Anonymous. The prayer was written by Reinhold Niebuhr, and the portion of the prayer that is most often recited reads this way: "God, grant me the serenity to accept the things

I cannot change, the courage to change the things I can, and the wisdom to know the difference."

If you have days when your mind seems to cycle through old concerns, you may find it helpful to distract yourself in a healthy way. Maybe you could hit golf balls at the driving range, see a funny movie, listen to music, window-shop, or call a friend. Putting your attention somewhere else for a while will interrupt your worry patterns and help you approach situations from a new perspective.

It is vital that we learn to break our cycles of worry and concern. If we don't, we will focus on those things we fear rather than on our positive goals.

Here are a few other tips that will help break the worry cycle.

- Remember to breathe and ground yourself in the present moment when you can't seem to calm your mind.

- Monitor your diet and notice if you suffer from anxiety after eating certain foods, like wheat, dairy products, nuts, or sugar. An allergic reaction or intolerance to these foods could aggravate your habit of worrying.

- Don't feel as if you have to solve all the world's problems. If you obsess about all the negativity you see on television or read in the papers, you aren't going to be able to help yourself, much less anyone else. Pick your cause and rally to it.

Trust that other people will feel guided to help with matters you don't have time for.

- Be selective about whom you spend time with. If you find that being around certain people makes you tired or worried, consider limiting the amount of time spent with them until you can be less sensitive to their fear and negativity.

Completing Unresolved Issues

All of us have unresolved issues that stem from past conflicts with other people. Sometimes these unresolved issues can last for years, and if we don't find a way to finally resolve them, they can affect us unconsciously and erode our attempts at gaining a lasting sense of peace.

Have you ever been going through your normal daily routine and suddenly had a thought about a past conflict? You remembered what the other person said to you, and then you thought of a comeback you wish you had uttered. Just as disconcerting is running into this person and realizing that attempts at being polite are unsuccessful. Deep inside, you are harboring resentment and can't be spontaneous, open, and honest. Because of this, you decide to avoid this person.

Situations like this pull us out of whatever level of joy and peace we have attained. Even if we decide not to see this person again, the unresolved conflict can surface and interfere with new relationships. Maybe we're fearful of repeating a negative pattern with a new acquaintance, so we start to close down. We limit our spontaneity again, afraid that this new relationship might turn out the same way. Old issues and resentments hang on and continue to affect us.

What do we do about these lingering issues? The answer lies in the age-old practice of forgiveness. Religious authorities all agree that there is something miraculous about the process of forgiveness. The act of forgiveness cleans the slate with people in ways no one can really explain. As we forgive ourselves and others, a transformation takes place that can be experienced and proved.

The first step is to be aware of any old conflicts and to begin the process by forgiving yourself. Get past the temptation to just replay what you might have said to put the person in his place. Without blaming yourself or others, consider how you could have handled the situation if you had only known what you know now. Keep in mind that you are a different person today and acknowledge any mistakes you made. Then let yourself off the hook. We are all souls in growth and we make mistakes. What's important is that we see our part in the conflict and then let it go.

These same rules apply when you are forgiving others. Review the situation and decide how you would have preferred it. Then consider the other person's point of view. This will give you insight into his behavior and allow you to give him the benefit of the doubt. He was probably doing the best he could with the knowledge he had at the time. He may even have his own regrets about his role in the conflict and is unsure of how to let you know.

The next step is to find a way to communicate with the other person so you can acknowledge the conflict and make amends. That can be done by making a phone call, talking in person, or writing a letter. Most people agree that this is the most difficult part of the process, but it is also the most healing. Remember, the purpose of resolving the old conflict is not to start up the relationship again, although that might occur. It is to put the situation to rest.

It is important to watch your own emotions and motivations. As an example, let's say you want to resolve a relationship that ended badly and you have decided to write a letter. You sit down and begin to write about how you wish the relationship had ended in a better way and that he or she meant a lot to you in the past. Then suddenly you feel old resentments coming up, preventing you from saying anything positive. Here my advice is to continue writing the letter. Get all your thoughts down on paper and then put the letter aside.

Now start a new letter and see if you can write it without anger or blame. Continue writing letters and putting them aside until you have one that is kind and to the point. Then decide if you want to mail it. The letter may have been more for your own clearing than for the benefit of the other person. Or it may be vital that the other person gets your letter in order for the forgiveness process to be complete. You will need to listen to your inner guidance to determine what's right for you.

Keep in mind that different people are going to respond to your attempts at making amends in different ways. Some people will be open and appreciative. Others may not be quite ready to let go of what happened. Either way, what is most important is that you make an attempt to clean up your past.

Just because you have made amends with someone doesn't mean you have to continue the relationship. Some people will naturally want more from us than we can give. Don't feel guilty if you choose to distance yourself. On the other hand, some relationships can be rekindled after a conflict is resolved and grow in incredibly meaningful ways. This seems to be especially true when old alienations are cleared up between parents and children or between siblings.

What about making amends with someone who has died or someone you are unable to find? In my opinion the forgiveness process is equally valuable. You can take the same steps and write a letter and later burn it as a gesture of completion. Or you can imagine the person standing in front of you and then tell him or her your regrets. Then you can give this person your blessing. Even if you don't believe your thoughts will go out and touch that person wherever he or she is, I think you will find that the process of forgiveness leaves you feeling peaceful and clear.

A Connection with the Sacred

The above activities set us up to connect with the most important source of our inner peace: the sacred. I am referring not only to our religious beliefs but also to a sense of the divine that is transcendent and assures us that there is a larger plan to life.

This kind of understanding means moving beyond the material aspects of our existence. We can have the right house, the perfect car, great vacation opportunities, and prestigious social recognition and still feel an emptiness inside. We can still find ourselves asking, "Is this all there is?"

Until we discover our true connection with the sacred, we will try to fill the hollow place inside with the constant pursuit of electronic toys, the perfect relationship, sports, or the need to shop. We might even try to medicate our emptiness with food, television, or various artificial stimulants. Or we might think, "If I could just find a way to have more fun, that would do it." Obviously there is nothing wrong with some of these activities in themselves. As stated before, they can help us escape our worries and preoccupations for a while so we can return with a clearer mind. But if we use them to make our lives feel worthwhile, they can become obsessions and self-destructive addictions. Most of all, they can't replace the longing we feel within our souls for a connection with a sacred source beyond this world. Spiritual texts encourage us to realize that this connection has to be more than just a belief. It must be experienced.

Such a connection first begins with the act of intention. We have to decide to pursue this experience. We have to knock on the door. We must actively seek to experience for ourselves what the great mystics have always told us: that God is in all things. That everything we see around us reflects some greater scheme. Our lives and all that has ever happened to us are part of it. With this realization, everything we experience deepens: Colors, people, art, and landscapes seem to stand out and become more beautiful. Everything we once took for granted has more presence as we sense its divinity.

At some point this experience shifts our sense of who we are, showing us that we are much more than we originally thought. We feel stronger and clearer about what to say and do. Ideas come more readily. We have hunches and intuitions that feel like an inner knowing. And we become more loving, peaceful, and content. The energy and peace of God look through our eyes.

As I mentioned at the beginning of this chapter, this connection with the sacred can happen anywhere: in prayer or meditation or while worshiping in church. It can also happen while walking along a trail in the beauty of nature, engaging in dance, practicing one of the martial arts, watching a baby smile, or talking to a special group of friends who are listening intently. Again, just having the intention for this experience can lead us to it.

Once it occurs, our connection with God feels like coming home. We no longer feel isolated in a universe that is meaningless and uncaring. Instead we feel the deep peace that comes from knowing we are loved and guided.

What is the best way to prepare for this experience? First we need to make the time. Set up your schedule so you aren't booked every moment. Take walks, meditate, or just wake up in the morning without any plans, then drift and see what happens. Spend time thinking about the bigger picture. Life is short and precious. We are all born and we make contributions to the world and then we leave, and a new generation takes over. Begin to get a sense of the grand design and your role in it.

As you learn to connect with a sense of the sacred, your ability to experience peace will evolve and deepen in ways you never imagined. You will also find that at first you tend to move in and out of this awareness. With practice you will increase your ability to maintain a peaceful state. In the meantime, when you find yourself worrying or becoming distracted by other, more worldly concerns, take a pause and draw upon your experience of the sacred.

❦❧

Meditation

This meditation is designed to help you have more inner peace by clearing the past and connecting with a sacred source.

During the meditation you will be asked to take a mental journey to a place that feels sacred to you. This could be a place of worship, an area in nature, or a special location from childhood. You might find it helpful to have the sacred site in mind before beginning.

As with all the meditations in this book, make sure you are in a quiet place where you won't be interrupted. Have a pen and paper nearby to write down any thoughts that come to you. Also remember to read each line or paragraph as a complete thought and finish the request before moving on to the next line.

Begin the meditation by taking a moment to become quiet and still . . .

Move your body around slightly to help it relax . . .

Take four slow, deep breaths . . .

Let your body relax and your mind become quiet . . .

Take a few more moments to be sure you are ready to move on . . .

Now let's begin our mental journey. Visualize yourself in front of a gate . . .

Notice the color of the gate . . .

Place your hand on it and feel what it is made of . . .

Push open the gate and look at the pathway in front of you . . .

Stroll along the pathway and notice your surroundings . . .

Continue as the path twists and turns, leading you to a special place . . .

Recognize this place as being very safe and sacred. It is your special place . . .

How would you describe this place? Are you in nature or in a beautiful building? . . .

Have you been here before, or is this a place you haven't yet experienced? . . .

Look at all the details . . .

Notice the colors . . .

Listen to the sounds . . .

Now find a comfortable spot to rest . . .

Enjoy the peacefulness of this place . . .

What makes it special and sacred to you? . . .

How do you feel being here? . . .

Breathe in the peacefulness . . .

For a moment, detach yourself from your ordinary perception of life. Expand your consciousness to feel that you are part of a bigger plan that is more important than your day-to-day concerns . . .

Consider that your life is guided by a spiritual source . . .

Feel at peace with this idea . . .

Let's use the peaceful feelings you have right now to help with issues you are currently dealing with in life.

Think about a current situation that prevents you from feeling peaceful at times . . .

Maybe you have been worrying lately about situations that you can't control or change . . .

Or maybe you have been worrying too much about possible future events . . .

How do you currently deal with this issue? . . .

What do you say to yourself when you think about this situation? . . .

How could you change your internal dialogue to give yourself more confidence when dealing with this issue? . . .

Would it help you to seek professional advice or counseling? . . .

What else could you do to find inner peace around this issue? . . .

Think about a time in the future when you will face this issue again . . .

What one thing could you do to help you stay centered when dealing with it? . . .

Feel as if you can handle this well . . .

Now let this issue go for a while and trust it is being taken care of . . .

Take a deep breath and notice your sacred surroundings again . . .

Take a moment to make sure you are still feeling peaceful before moving on . . .

Now focus on a relationship from the past that either didn't end well or was affected by a disagreement . . .

Choose one that you are ready to heal . . .

Who is the person, and what was the conflict about? . . .

Have the difficulties of this relationship ever entered your mind and troubled you? . . .

Would it help ease your mind to have closure? . . .

If that person were standing in front of you right now, what could you say that would be healing for both of you? Take your time to really think through this question . . .

Is there anything you would like to hear this person say to you? . . .

Is there anything else you would like to say to him or her? . . .

Experience the conversation going well and the other person acknowledging your healing words . . .

Now imagine that you have made your amends. How much more freedom will you feel? . . .

Will your thoughts be more hopeful when you think about this person in the future? . . .

For now, turn this process over to a higher power. Feel that when you are ready, you will know exactly what to do to make amends . . .

Take a moment to breathe and focus on your sacred place again . . .

Enjoy the peaceful beauty . . .

Anchor in the peacefulness you feel by choosing a special symbol that will remind you of this experience. Anytime you think about this symbol or actually see it, you will be reminded to feel peaceful . . .

What is your symbol? . . .

When you are ready, prepare to leave this sacred place, knowing you can return anytime you like . . .

Make your way back along the pathway you followed in . . .

Notice the gate in the distance and move toward it . . .

Move through the gate, closing it behind you . . .

Focus again on your physical body. Move it around slightly.

Be alert over the next few days to ideas that come to you, and keep in mind that anytime you feel your mind becoming distracted by worries, you can center yourself in quick, healthy ways. And consider turning your worries over to a higher power.

SUGGESTED READING

Chop Wood, Carry Water: A Guide to Finding Spiritual Fulfillment in Everyday Life. Rick Fields. Jeremy P. Tarcher, 1984.

Good News for Bad Days: Living a Soulful Life. Father Paul Keenan. Warner Books, 1998.

Beyond Golf: How to Transform Your Game and Your Life. Larry Miller. Stillpoint Publishing, 1996.

New Low Blood Sugar and You. Carlton Fredericks, Ph.D. Perigee Books, 1985.

Prayer Is Good Medicine: How to Reap the Healing Benefits of Prayer. Larry Dossey. HarperCollins, 1997.

Saved by the Light: The True Story of a Man Who Died Twice and the Profound Revelations He Received. Dannion Brinkley. Harper, 1995.

Sick and Tired? Reclaim Your Inner Terrain. Robert O. Young, Ph.D., D.Sc. Woodbridge, 1999.

The Way of the Peaceful Warrior. Dan Millman. H. J. Kramer, 1985.

Peace Is Every Step: The Path of Mindfulness in Everyday Life. Thich Nhat Hanh. Bantam Books, 1992.

CHAPTER SIX

The Miracle of Synchronicity

❧

Life is full of coincidences. We stumble upon a new job or business opportunity or mysteriously meet someone who becomes our partner, confidant, or spouse. We may dream about an old friend one night and the next day find that person knocking on our front door. Just as intriguing are the times when the phone rings and we intuitively know who is calling. Similarly, most people can remember a time when they made a decision to do something like buy a new car or seek out a new career, and soon after, information or people coincidentally came into their lives to help make that dream come true.

Take, for example, a story told by Wayne Dyer in his book *You'll See It When You Believe It.* He relates a remarkable event that happened to him while trying to find his estranged father, who abandoned his family when Wayne was a small child. One day Wayne received a call from a distant relative telling him that his father had died six years earlier and was buried in Biloxi, Mississippi. Four years after the phone call, Wayne was on business in a town in Mississippi that was about two hundred miles from Biloxi. He decided to rent a car and drive there to see his father's grave.

The car that Wayne rented was new and had never been driven before. The seat belts hadn't even been unwrapped and removed from under the car seat. To get to the seat belt, Wayne took the seat out of the car, ripped off the plastic casing, and opened the buckle. Inside, to his surprise, was a business card that read, "Candlelight Inn, Biloxi, Mississippi." Also printed on the card were the address and telephone number, along with directions. Wayne slipped the card into his shirt pocket and drove on.

Once in Biloxi, he stopped at a service station to search through the phone book for the local cemeteries. Not knowing where his father was buried, he called one of the cemeteries, hoping someone could help him. The first person he spoke with was an elderly man who confirmed that Wayne's father was buried there. Before Wayne could ask for directions, the man said, "Your father is buried adjacent to the grounds of the Candlelight Inn. Just ask someone at the station how to get there." In awe, Wayne reached into his shirt pocket to retrieve the Candlelight Inn business card. From the directions on the back he could tell he was only three blocks from the cemetery.

Such coincidences occur with frequency to all of us and have now been documented by scientists, most notably the early-twentieth-century Swiss psychologist Carl Jung. Jung termed this phenomenon "synchronicity," which he defined as meaningful coincidences. Based on his personal experience and the experiences of his clients, Jung came to believe that there is an ordering force or principle in the universe that acts to guide us toward a certain destiny. Most of us call this force God. Jung also believed this force was alive in every person's life and that all we have to do is look for it, open up to the sacred, and begin to act on the opportunities that are presented.

Intuition

How do these synchronistic events take place? Many times they begin with an intuition, a thought or feeling to do something or go somewhere. For instance, we might be heading to work one day, with a long list of things to do, and suddenly have a thought to stop by the bookstore first.

Our rational minds might dismiss the idea as a waste of valuable time and urge us to get to the office. Yet when we decide to follow the hunch and stop at the bookstore, we meet someone or find a book that solves a problem we've been having at work. In this case the coincidence of finding a much-needed solution came as a result of listening to an intuition.

Most synchronicities seem to take this form. First we have an intuition, and then, if we follow it, we experience a synchronistic event that makes our lives better or leads us in a different direction. This is why it's wise to use intuition along with logic when making decisions. Instead of relying just on logic and staying focused only on what's scheduled, we need to listen to the ideas that pop into our minds.

Here is an example of how one man's intuition changed his life and the lives of others. The man's name was Greg O'Leary, and his story is from the book *Small Miracles*, by Yitta Halberstam and Judith Leventhal.

One night when walking home, Greg had an urge to take a completely new and different route. Along the way, he heard the sounds of a struggle in a clump of bushes a few yards off the sidewalk. By the muffled screams and tearing of clothing he could tell that a woman was being attacked. For a few seconds Greg deliberated about whether or not to call the police or to intervene. Even though he didn't consider himself strong or brave, he decided that he must help the woman even if it meant being hurt himself. He ran to the bushes and pulled the man off the woman. After resisting for a few moments the assailant ran off.

In the darkness Greg could see the outline of a young woman

crouched behind a tree, sobbing. To reassure her, he said, "It's okay, the man ran away. You're safe now."

After a long pause, the young woman said, "Dad, is that you?" When the woman then came out from behind the tree, Greg saw she was his youngest daughter, Katherine.

If followed, our intuitions cannot only save lives but also guide us into making major decisions. A few years ago I interviewed Larry Kirshbaum, chairman of the board at Warner Books (the company that has published this book). I asked him how he made decisions on which books to publish. Knowing that thousands of manuscripts are submitted to his company annually, I was curious as to how he determined which ones would sell and which ones wouldn't. His response was that he used certain criteria in evaluating books, and once that evaluation was made, he relied heavily on his intuition to guide him.

Using intuition in business and science is nothing new. Some of the leading thinkers in history have followed their intuition to make their greatest discoveries and accomplishments. Doctors and nurses often report using their intuition when making decisions about their patients. One such doctor told his story in the book *Practical Intuition*, by Laura Day. The physician wrote that while eating lunch one day he had a sense that something was wrong with the thyroid gland of a patient he was scheduled to see later that afternoon. He made a mental note of his feelings but wasn't sure if there was any truth to his hunch, since he had never met the woman.

The woman came to him for a routine examination and appeared to be healthy. The doctor decided to perform a series of thyroid tests anyway. When the laboratory results came in, they seemed to indicate a problem, and he referred her to a specialist who discovered a nodule on her thyroid. Fortunately her illness was treated before there were any complications.

Increasing Intuition

The results of following our intuition will often amaze us and leave us wanting more. Even though the way these guiding thoughts arrive is still a mystery, increasing them may merely be a matter of paying more attention to our urges and our vision of the future. Affirming what we see and prayerfully asking for more insightful intuition is also helpful.

As we carefully watch our thoughts, we can readily detect two kinds coming into our minds. The thoughts we use to analyze and assess our everyday circumstances are one type. We use this way of thinking when we drive up to a parking place and think about the size of our car and whether we can park it in the space provided. We judge and analyze.

Intuition represents the other kind of thinking. It is thought that we don't intentionally "think." It just seems to occur, arriving in a sense in the back of our minds. It almost always pertains to something that we should do or say. It feels like a spontaneous idea that comes out of the blue and suggests a change of course, even if a minor one. Sometimes the thoughts that spring from intuition seem as though they aren't as logical and strategically obvious as our more analytical thoughts.

True intuition can guide us. It is about growing and expanding and putting ourselves in the right place at the right time for something helpful and perhaps destined to occur. These thoughts will feel positive and hopeful and are often surrounded by a sense of inspiration or excitement.

If we watch closely, intuition will always pertain to real questions that we have about our lives. If we keep our sacred connections strong and stay observant, we will begin to see our lives as a story unfolding. From this perspective we will be able to detect certain questions that are relevant to what is happening in our lives. These questions will be general at times, such as whether we should stay in our current job or look for something else. At other times they will be quite specific, such as "Which way should I walk home?" as in Greg's story. In any case, what's important is that we ask our questions as specifically as possible and stay open to the answer. We may have a thought that inspires us, or we could bump into someone who could help us. Or maybe we will get a glimpse of going somewhere or doing something that puts us in the perfect position for an important coincidence to take place.

Here is an example of what happened to me when I asked

the right question. It took place in the spring of 1997 when I was driving to Sedona, Arizona, from Santa Fe, New Mexico, with my friend Jimmi.

We had rented a car from the Hertz rental car agency and were about thirty minutes outside of Santa Fe when we decided to listen to an audiocassette. The topic of the tape was how the events in our lives give us opportunities to grow. The speaker on the tape was saying that there will be times when we are faced with circumstances that we may not like or even understand but they will always provide us with an opportunity to learn about life and ourselves.

In his list of potential challenges the speaker mentioned acts of nature. Just as he finished the words "acts of nature" a strong gust of wind rocked our car. Jimmi and I looked out the window and saw an old scrap-metal car door flying toward the passenger side of the car. It hit the car, pierced the right front tire, and cracked the tire frame. Jimmi and I were in shock. It had happened so quickly.

I immediately pulled the car over and looked at Jimmi. Without saying a word we burst into laughter. Once Jimmi caught her breath, she said, "I can't believe it. The speaker on the tape was just talking about events like that."

We sat there a moment, being grateful that neither one of us had been hurt. Then we spotted a car about half a mile up the road that had pulled over. We thought the driver had stopped to help us, so we started walking toward him. Just as we were halfway there, the car sped away. Jimmi and I couldn't believe he had driven off. There we were in the desert, thirty miles from the nearest town, with a wrecked car and no cellular phone. And the wind had picked up again, making it impossible for us to walk for help.

Not knowing what else to do, I suddenly said aloud, "Okay, God, what do you want me to do?" At that exact moment a tow truck pulled up and stopped. Out stepped a man with the word "Hertz" lettered across his lapel. He just happened to be on his way from Santa Fe to the Hertz rental office in Albuquerque and recognized our car as belonging to his company. He stopped because he thought we might need help.

Taking Advantage of Synchronicity

Staying open to the coincidences in life can leave us with miraculous opportunities. But just following our intuition and noticing mysterious coincidences is not enough. There is one more step. We have to take advantage of the synchronicity.

Following our hunches, we will be led to the right place at the right time. And sometimes that right place is within earshot of a conversation that provides us with valuable information.

Denise Linn in her book *The Secret Language of Signs* relates a story of a woman named Carol. While waiting in the checkout line at the grocery store, Carol overheard two women talking about automobile tires. The women were saying that sometimes tires develop bulges and then blow out on the highway, causing serious accidents. Carol never looked at her tires or even gave them any thought. However, when she went out to the parking lot with her groceries, she looked at her tires and discovered a large ballooning spot on one of them. She drove to the nearest service station to have someone look at the tire. Once there, she was told how lucky it was that she came in when she did. Because of the damage to the tire, it could have burst at any moment.

The true value in Carol overhearing the conversation came when she acted on what she heard. Had she not taken the time to consider what the women were saying, she might have found herself in an accident.

Other synchronicities are harder to act upon. What if you had a spontaneous thought, for instance, about going to the mall to do some shopping? You could go later, but because the intuitive thought occurred, you decide to go now. As you enter the mall, you notice a particular person going into the building at the same time. This may not be significant except that later, in a store at the mall, you discover the same person standing right beside you looking at a rack of clothes. And if that isn't enough, to your amazement, at noon you discover that the two of you are eating in the same restaurant.

Clearly a synchronicity of some kind is occurring. But wh

do you make of it? In this example we can see that just following your intuition and noticing a mysterious coincidence is not
enough. You have to find out what the message is. In this case
you could find a way to strike up a conversation and see what
the other person might say. You have no idea what could occur.
It might pertain to a question you are working on or to some
other aspect of your life with which you are in need of help. The
important point is to explore the opportunity to communicate
with this person.

Sometimes synchronicity requires action of a different kind.
You may have the thought to go somewhere, and when you arrive, nothing of note occurs. Perhaps you are at a pub that is almost empty, and the only other information source is a
television. Don't completely overlook a bit of information that
might be coming across that medium. Pay attention to what is
being said; it could be synchronistic. The same can be said of
other information sources. You might glance up and notice a
book or magazine, and if you take a closer look, there could be
a story or news item that contains exactly the information you
need at that point in your life.

Often the synchronistic messages come to us in ways we
expect. We could be driving down the highway and see a
reads, "Isn't it time you took a vacation?" This may
ything on a typical day. However, on this day we
n asking ourselves if it was time to take a vaca-
the message, we may find that the travel agent

we call has a fabulous deal on a trip to the destination we had in mind, and the deal became available moments before we called.

Other interesting forms of synchronistic messages come when lights blink at the precise moment something important is said, a clock radio spontaneously turns on, blaring a song that contains the message someone is seeking, or a friend calls a friend when she is most needed. These messages might be passed off as coincidences if someone doesn't trust that life-enhancing messages can come from a variety of sources. If acknowledged, many of these strange encounters will prove worthy of our time and attention.

My friend Savann made a remarkable discovery one day when she paid attention to the small messages that people sometimes overlook. She was at home writing one morning when the phone rang. It was her daughter calling to say that her black leather tote bag had been taken from her car while she was a guest at a dinner party the night before. The tote bag contained a wallet, a cell phone, eyeglasses, and other items along with her address book, which was filled with unlisted telephone numbers and addresses of friends and business associates.

Savann hung up the phone and sat at her computer for a moment. Out of frustration and anger for her daughter's loss, she began to speak out loud. With strong emotion she said, "All right, you can have the cash and credit cards, but under no circumstances can you have the rest of her belongings, especially her address book . . . so return them *now*!" After she finished speaking, the computer screen in front of her went blank.

Savann's car keys were lying on her desk in front of her. Suddenly she picked up the keys and headed for the car, again demanding, "Show me where the tote bag is."

As if the car were on automatic pilot, it passed a sign directing Savann straight ahead and then another sign that read No Left Turn. She turned right. Coming to a sign that read Slow, the car turned the corner and began down a long winding road, crossing a bridge. There, beside the road, lying in the grass, was the black leather tote bag. The only items missing were the cash and credit cards.

Like Savann, when we act on our strong urges and believe we are guided, amazing events will take place. Our determination to have more of these events in our lives and our willingness to explore the messages we receive can strengthen our belief and acceptance of the higher force that is leading our lives forward, on a miraculous journey.

Meditation

This meditation is designed to help you become more aware of the synchronistic events in your life, and not only to trust them but also to begin to have more of them.

Before you begin the meditation, find a quiet, comfortable place where you can have about fifteen minutes of uninterrupted time. Be sure to read each line or paragraph as a complete thought before moving on to the next line.

Spend a few moments getting quiet and comfortable . . .

Squeeze and contract any tense muscles to help your body relax . . .

Take four slow breaths, feeling your chest and stomach expand and contract . . .

Let all your cares and concerns drift by . . .

Slowly count to ten . . .

Take a few more seconds to quiet your mind and relax your body . . .

111

Now that you are relaxed, think about times in the past when you have had an intuition about something and it was later confirmed . . .

Think of a time when the phone rang and you knew who was on the other end of the line . . .

Have you ever had a passing thought about someone and soon after, the person called or you ran into him somewhere? . . .

Have you had an intuition regarding family members? Maybe you felt something special was about to happen to them and it did. Or you could have thought one of them was not feeling well or had been in an accident, and you were right . . .

What is the difference in your intuitive thoughts and a random thought? . . .

What about the remarkable coincidences that have taken place in your life? Can you remember one or two of them? . . .

Did these events move you toward a new direction, introduce you to new people that are now important to you, or help you find the perfect place to live? . . .

Did your intuition play a role in the synchronistic events? . . .

What did you say to yourself when these events took place? . . .

How did you feel or what did you think when these events occurred? How did they affect your life and your belief that you are guided? . . .

Did these events build your confidence so you would begin to expect them to happen more often? . . .

What do you think would need to happen in order for you to experience more synchronicity? . . .

To build your trust and to give you practice in enhancing synchronicity, let's walk through a typical day and observe how you can increase the coincidences in your life.

Imagine that it is morning and you are waking up in your normal way, only today you are full of an expectation that something mysterious will take place . . .

In order to experience the mysterious, you will need to have a primary question for the day in mind. Maybe you are looking for an answer to a problem like how to end a relationship, how to strengthen a relationship, or how to pay off your bills. Or maybe you want to know which car to buy or which job to accept. It can be any kind of question regarding what's currently happening in your life . . .

What would your question be? . . .

Imagine that you have your question in mind as you go through your routine of getting ready to go out . . .

If you watch the news or listen to the radio, keep your question in mind and listen for any information that might be related to it . . .

As you leave the house, notice whom you come across . . .

On your way to work, school, or the market, notice the street signs and advertisements around you. Look for any hidden messages that might apply to your question . . .

At lunchtime imagine going to a certain restaurant. Notice if you coincidentally run into someone or if you overhear a conversation that helps you . . .

Move through your day with your question in mind, noticing all the ways answers can come to you . . .

When you return home, have some fun and go on a mini vision quest around your yard or neighborhood. Pick up any pieces of paper or small objects that might have meaning to you . . .

Once home, look over the items and read the messages you picked up. Look carefully for hidden meanings . . .

Reflect back over the day and look for ways that your answers might have come . . .

Now think about your next few days. How could you start each of these days with a predominant question in mind? . . .

Where would you go to find answers? . . .

Spend a few more moments thinking about your questions. Pay attention to any intuitive thoughts you have . . .

When you are ready, return to present time with your question in mind . . .

Move your body around slightly . . .

Make a few notes . . .

And return to your day.

Over the next few weeks, as you keep your main question in mind while going through your days, accept all forms of information that come to you, even if some appear to be silly. Look for a hidden meaning in street signs, scrap pieces of paper lying around, or news articles. These items may or may not have helpful clues, but you may miss something if you aren't open to the mysterious possibilities of synchronistic events.

SUGGESTED READING

Intuition Workout. Nancy Rosanoff. Aslan Publishing, 1988.

Practical Intuition. Laura Day. Broadway Books, 1997.

Small Miracles. Yitta Halberstam and Judith Leventhal. Adams Media Group, 1997.

The Secret Language of Signs. Denise Linn. Ballantine Books, 1996.

CHAPTER SEVEN

Discovering Your Spiritual Mission

❧

Once we attune to the synchronicity in our lives, we see that mysterious coincidences are leading us in a particular direction: toward some service or mission to help make the world a better place. I believe we are all born with a spiritual mission, and once we awaken to it, our lives take on a higher meaning. Psychologists call this perception "self-actualization," or the fulfillment of inner potential.

In his book *Man's Search for Meaning* Viktor Frankl expresses the idea of spiritual mission in this way: "Everyone has his own specific vocation or mission in life to carry out a concrete assignment which demands fulfillment. Therein he cannot be replaced, nor can his life be repeated. Thus everyone's task is as unique as his specific opportunity to implement it."

Ari Kiev, M.D., emphasizes the importance of mission in his

book *A Strategy for Daily Living* by saying, "In thirty-five years of psychiatric practice, I have repeatedly found that helping people to develop personal visions has proven to be the most effective way to help them cope with problems and maximize their satisfactions."

There is an emptiness that goes along with not living our spiritual purpose. Often, as we have discussed, we try to distract ourselves from the longings inside. Fortunately our souls continue to nudge us until we find a way to recognize the mission we have come to the world to undertake.

Sometimes a personal crisis catapults us toward our mission. The death of a loved one, an illness, a divorce, or a sudden career change can leave us searching for something solid. The reality of the impermanence of life can hit us hard, making us question what we can rely on. Some people, unable to find a transcendent purpose, may even feel their lives are over and contemplate suicide. When this happens, we are experiencing what poets have called the "dark night of the soul." It is a time when things seem their worst. What once gave us comfort and safety is no longer enough. Yet, just as the darkest part of night comes before dawn, so does the darkest fear of life often come before the joy of discovering our spiritual mission. In a sense we are merely waking up and restructuring our lives to be more whole.

Just as finding a spiritual connection is an individual process, so too is the journey toward understanding spiritual mission.

118

Some people are born with a clear awareness of what they want to do with their lives. They plot a course and continuously work toward fulfilling their mission. Others won't even be interested in their mission until later in life. They go through much of their lives striving for what everyone says is important, until one day they begin to question whether or not there is something more.

The journey toward greater understanding of mission can be found in a variety of ways. Some people turn to the spiritual messages of their religion. Others adopt the rich traditions of cultures like the Native American. And others choose self-help seminars and counseling.

Even though our approaches to spiritual mission are individualized, there are similarities in all methods of searching. In all cases we can listen to the deep knowing we have inside that tells us what we are here to do. This knowing is connected to our interests, the images we see, and the gut reactions we have toward a particular area or vocation in life that seems most desirable and fun. "Wow," we might say when we imagine working within a certain field. We may even remark, "If only I could do that, my dreams would come true."

As mentioned in Chapter Two, we sometimes think this type of dreaming can only take place in childhood. Once adults, we believe we have to settle for the jobs or opportunities we can get, rather than the ones we most want. This often limits our ability to stay connected with our deeper intuitive vision of what we are here to do. Remember that people change jobs and careers all the time in order to follow their dreams. It is never too late.

Exploring Your Past

Gaining clarity on your mission also comes from a deep exploration of your past. Using your understanding of the sacredness of life, you can uncover the spiritual meaning behind all that has occurred. Just think about the circumstances of your birth. What is the meaning behind being born to your particular parents, in that particular part of the world, during this particular time in history?

No one has ever been on the earth before who has had your same experiences or distinct view of the world. Your uniqueness began with your parents or primary caregivers and their expressions of life. What did you learn from them? What did their lives seem to be about?

Here you may want to be careful to get past any resentments that developed from childhood situations. Most of us will find that the mistakes our parents made were honest and that they were doing the best that they knew how. Even though we may not agree with what happened, and we don't want to see it repeated for our children, we realize we can't change that part of our past. The best thing to do is to learn from the experiences and use them to help others.

Find the most positive aspects of the people around you in your early family. What abilities did they have that you were attracted to? Was there an occupation that was common? As an example, your family might have been involved with the field of healing. There may have been doctors, nurses, and physical therapists. If you have carried on the tradition, could it now be your turn to evolve the occupation to a higher form?

Many people discover that they have been influenced by avocations and hobbies that were enjoyed by other family members. Some examples are cooking, photography, traveling, and gardening. Can these interests now be utilized in a special way?

My parents influenced my passion for writing. They loved English literature and both taught English at the university level. I can't remember a time when one of them wasn't reading or discussing a book. And having published authors in my family has made being a writer an accessible occupation.

As you search through your past, remember to consider your innate abilities and talents. Think about the dreams of the future you had as a child. What did you want to be when you grew up? Which teachers did you love during your childhood and adolescence, and how did they influence you? Which subjects did you enjoy?

Also look for a connection between your current lifestyle and the activities that you explored as a child. And what about the first few jobs you held? How have they led to the other employment you've had in your life?

The final step is looking at your life story as a whole. See as clearly as possible the meaning behind all that has occurred—from the dreams and upsets of your early childhood through the mistakes, dead ends, joys, and triumphs of adolescence and adulthood. What did all of this prepare you to teach others about what's important in leading a fuller, more spiritual life?

Such reflection will reveal a simple truth that is yours to tell. And that's where a sense of mission starts. From there you can find a way to expand your current activities and goals in the direction of telling this truth.

Let me share with you the story of one woman who used her childhood trauma to become a leader in the field of recovery and addiction. Marsha was born in the early 1950s to alcoholic parents. She spent much of her childhood taking care of her parents and learning how to cope in an unstable environment.

As a teenager Marsha worked at a local fast-food restaurant. Her goal was to save enough money to pay for her college education. Because she was a compassionate listener, her coworkers began seeing her as their counselor and going to her for advice. One male coworker asked her for help with handling a problem he was having with his girlfriend, who was an alcoholic. Marsha understood his pain and decided to go with him to the local halfway house to visit the girlfriend.

While there, Marsha had an intuition that she would benefit

from volunteering a few hours a week at the halfway house. She wanted to major in psychology and minor in sociology, and she felt that being in that environment might help prepare her for college.

After six months of volunteer work, Marsha was offered a job by the director of the halfway house. She accepted the position and found herself flourishing. A year later the director invited Marsha to attend a statewide conference on addiction and recovery, at which the director was giving a lecture on how to help families of alcoholics, and she thought Marsha's testimony would be beneficial.

After the lecture several people came up to Marsha and thanked her for her input. One woman told her about a scholarship program that was being offered in the field of psychology with an emphasis on addiction and recovery, and suggested that she apply. Marsha applied for the scholarship and got it. After graduation she attended graduate school and got her Ph.D.

Eventually Marsha became the director of a clinic in a city not far from where she grew up. She turned the clinic into a healing center that provided support for people recovering from alcohol addiction as well as other addictions. She was one of the first directors in her field to provide her patients access to biofeedback, massage therapy, and homeopathic remedies, as well as inviting motivational speakers to talk regularly. She even wrote a manual about her work that set a standard in her field.

It is easy to see how Marsha's life experience prepared her

for her spiritual mission. She wasn't content with the old recovery model, and she knew firsthand the pain of being a child of an alcoholic. Synchronistically guided, she went with a coworker to a halfway house, and her destiny began to unfold.

Taking Your Mission into the World

To expand your sense of mission, I suggest that you first write down what you believe it to be. Distill your truth into as simple a statement as possible. Review it from time to time and play with the words until it feels right to you. Seeing something on paper in your own handwriting makes it more real.

For greater clarity ask questions, like "What was I born to do?" or "How can I help the world with my mission today?" After asking these questions, some people are surprised to learn that their mission is to make people feel better about themselves. Maybe they are the ones who always have a joke to tell. Or they love to cook for the neighbor down the street who is ill.

Other people will realize that demonstrating the equality between different races is their mission. They grew up within a culture that respected diversity and now they want to share that message. Or they saw so much prejudice when they were growing up that they are determined not to let it continue. Still others will be involved in some way with protecting the environment or making a scientific breakthrough. All of these spiritual missions could take a thousand forms based on the way an individual expresses his or her special vision.

Lawrence LeShan brings some clarity to the expression of mission in his book *Cancer as a Turning Point*. In helping a recovering cancer patient named Harold understand his dream occupation, LeShan asked Harold to express what he wanted to do with his life. Harold said that his lifelong dream was to be a physician, but since he was sixty-two and only had a high school education, he didn't think it was possible.

Knowing the connection between having a purpose in life and healing, LeShan urged Harold to explore why he wanted to be a physician. He asked Harold what being a physician meant. Harold said it meant having an office where a steady flow of people come in, get advice, and leave feeling better.

Based on this definition, Harold and LeShan were able to find the perfect job for Harold. He started working at a tourist information booth in a resort area. He would sit in the booth and a steady flow of people would come in daily to see him. They would ask for help in finding the right hotel and vacation spot in the area. Harold would give them advice and even ask them questions to clarify what they wanted in a vacation. Everyone who came to see him left feeling better. Without spending years in medical school, Harold was able to be of service in a way that met the needs he had thought to fulfill by being a physician.

A message that can come from Harold's experience is that if

a door closes, preventing us from pursuing our mission, we can look for other avenues for reaching our goal. We aren't limited in the way we can express our spiritual mission. We don't have to be doctors, celebrities, or leaders of our country in order to make the world a better place. As Theodore Roosevelt said, "Do what you can with what you have, where you are."

Don't worry if your current job seems very removed from your current sense of mission. From a spiritual perspective, you can assume that your current career is in some way part of your preparation. Spend time thinking about how, like Harold, you could fulfill some aspect of your mission within your current employment situation. It may require rearranging your priorities, changing the values in your office, or stretching the parameters of normal practice within your profession.

You will also find ways to actualize your mission in your avocational life. Perhaps you are still in college or between jobs, or you have chosen to be a homemaker. In these and other cases synchronicity can bring situations and opportunities before you to tell your truth. Within the vast spectrum of volunteer opportunities, as well as within the responsibilities of our own families, we can find a way to make our communities better.

Evolving Your Mission

Remember, your mission is your focus in life, not just a particular job. Often we get hung up thinking, "I am a schoolteacher" or "I am an attorney." Identifying with our jobs can become a problem at a certain point in our lives. What happens when it's time to retire or we decide to change careers? Who are we then?

Take, for example, what happened to Pilar, a successful soccer player in South America. He helped his team win numerous championships and awards. At thirty he felt at the top of his game. He thought his mission was to represent his country and to be the best soccer player ever. He was rich, famous, and loved by his countrymen.

His career as a soccer player seemed as if it would only expand. Then he broke his foot during a championship playoff, and even after surgery, he found himself unable to play soccer at the professional level.

Without the game, Pilar felt lost. He doubted whether he could find anything that would inspire him as much as soccer. He had acquired a broad knowledge of the history and practice of the game, and he thought all that experience was now wasted. However, within a year he was offered a job as a TV commentator, and he went on to have a long career as a broadcaster and lecturer. He also spent time as a volunteer coach for a local youth soccer team. His true mission was to promote the "zone" experience that comes from playing soccer, and for him, playing was just the first stage.

Pilar's experience is a reminder that our sense of mission will continue to be redefined and clarified throughout our lives. Our first attempts will always lead to more efficient and meaningful ways to express our truths.

What's most important is that we be able to step back at the end of our lives with pride in what we have accomplished. As George Bernard Shaw said, "This is the true joy in life . . . being used for a purpose recognized by yourself as a mighty one; . . . being a force of Nature instead of a feverish selfish little clod of ailments and grievances complaining that the world will not devote itself to making you happy." Later in life, Shaw went on to say, "I am of the opinion that my life belongs to the whole community and as long as I live it is my privilege to do for it whatsoever I can . . . Life is no 'brief candle' to me. It is a sort of splendid torch which I have got hold of for the moment; and I want to make it burn as brightly as possible before handing it on to future generations."

How do you want to be remembered? What do you want to leave the world? As your mission is clarified with time and consistency, you will know your importance. You have something to do and say that no one else can express. You have untapped gifts that will continue to come to light until your final days here on earth. Each time a gift is unveiled and put to use, you help make the world a better place for us all.

❧☙

Meditation

This meditation is designed to help you understand your spiritual mission by listening to your hopes and dreams. It is an exciting meditation because it can help you see your life in a new way and then lead you to the next step.

My suggestion is that you take plenty of time to complete the exercise and that you do the meditation more than once. Each time you do it, you will gain greater awareness.

As with all the meditations in this book, it is important that you be in a quiet, comfortable environment before beginning. Also remember to complete the request of each line or paragraph before reading the next line.

Begin the meditation by moving your body around slightly to help it relax . . .

Take a few deep breaths and feel yourself letting go . . .

Put all your concerns to the side for a while . . .

Spend about fifteen more seconds preparing . . .

Now let's take a mental journey together . . .

Imagine that you are on a special holiday at the beach . . .

Look out at the calm, clear water of the ocean . . .

Notice how beautiful it is . . .

Feel the sand . . .

Smell the air . . .

Listen to the seagulls flying overhead . . .

Feel the warm sun on your body . . .

Now imagine that you are no longer an adult. You are actually a happy child who loves to play at the beach . . .

Embody the essence of a child and begin to play in the water and sand . . .

Explore for a while until you find a few shells and sand dollars. Put them in your bucket . . .

Continue to play. Make this a joyful experience . . .

Feel loved and protected on this holiday . . .

When you feel you have really connected with the joy of being a child, ask yourself what someone this age would feel to be his or her purpose in life . . .

Listen for an answer . . .

Make a mental note of what you heard, and let's move forward in age . . .

Imagine that you are now a strong, healthy teenager . . .

Enjoy the beach the way you would as a teenager . . .

Feel all the hopes and dreams that come with being this age . . .

What do you at this age feel is your purpose in life? . . .

Without questioning the response, listen for answers . . .

Keeping the responses in mind, move forward in time to your current age . . .

Enjoy the beach by playing in the sand and water more joyfully than you can remember doing in years . . .

Feel free . . .

Laugh and smile . . .

Ask yourself what you feel is now your spiritual purpose . . .

Listen respectfully to your responses . . .

Think back on your life and notice any events that led you to this current spiritual purpose . . .

Were there key people you met along the way? . . .

Were there events that made you become more than you originally thought you could be? . . .

Were there jobs and volunteer positions that prepared you? . . .

What have all your experiences in the past led you to do currently? . . .

Spend a few moments thinking about the patterns of the past and how each of them has been a preparation . . .

Now let's move forward in time . . .

Imagine you are much older and wiser . . .

Continue to feel strong and healthy and enjoy the beach at this age . . .

If at this age you were to reflect back on your life, what would you feel was one of your greatest contributions to the world? . . .

What else would you have done that you were proud of? . . .

What will you at this age say is your spiritual mission? . . .

Listen carefully to all the responses . . .

Now return to your current age . . .

Is there a way that you can implement some of the messages you heard from yourself at various ages, to enhance your current spiritual mission? . . .

There is a final question. Is there any desire you have deep within your heart that you are not currently expressing? . . .

How could this be connected to your mission? . . .

Take a few more moments to think about all you have uncovered in this self-exploration, and how your hopes and dreams as a child and teenager have influenced what you want to share with the world today . . .

Prepare to end your holiday at the ocean . . .

When you are ready, move your body around slightly to signal that you have finished the meditation . . .

Take a few deep breaths . . .

And continue with your day.

Remember, whatever age you are, you have your whole life in front of you to express yourself. Use your time and resources to create a life that benefits you and others. That is where you will find your greatest joy.

SUGGESTED READING

Man's Search for Meaning. Viktor Frankl. Pocket Books, 1959.

Cancer as a Turning Point. Lawrence LeShan, Ph.D. Penguin Books, 1989.

The Purpose of Your Life. Carol Adrienne. Eagle Brook, 1998.

The Power of Purpose: Creating Meaning in Your Life and Work. Richard J. Leider. Berrett-Koehler Publishers, 1997.

The Tenth Insight. James Redfield. Warner Books, 1997.

Voices from the Heart: In Celebration of America's Volunteers. Brian O'Connell. Chronicle Books, 1999.

CHAPTER EIGHT

Making Joy a Lifestyle

❧❧

The purpose of this book is to guide you toward making joy a lifestyle. Joyful living needs to be more than just a good idea. It has to become an attitude that is thoroughly integrated into our day-to-day activities. The components for this way of living must be embraced fully as a matter of practice.

We can begin with a strong intention. We must desire to have joy in our lives and consistently hold a vision of the experience. We will want to be aware of how having more joy will change our lives. In this sense we must see ourselves turning the page and beginning a new chapter in our life story. This is why, as we discussed in Chapter One, releasing the pain and disappointment of the past is so important. It allows us to move beyond painful memories that hold us back. As we identify the past experiences that trigger resentment, jealousy, anger, or hurt, we can ask ourselves, "What do I need to do to release this experience?" or "How can I heal this emotion?"

The answer always lies in forgiveness. Forgive others, yourself, even life, for all that has happened to you. Once you are willing to forgive, you will be synchronistically led toward the best way to grow. It may come from interacting with a support group or a therapist, or you might find your answers in a recovery book or from a loving friend who has been through a similar experience. Whatever the means, it is possible to change the way we view our past and to see every aspect of our life story as a preparation for what is coming next.

Keep in mind that releasing the past and moving toward joy doesn't mean we will no longer face life challenges. We will still encounter events that seem like obstacles. People we care about will become ill and die, money management will still be necessary no matter what our income level is, and someone will come along and push our buttons when we least expect it.

The bottom line is that whether or not our lives are characterized by joy is a choice. It is up to us to clear our emotional baggage and to manage our reactions to all situations. Instead of allowing painful events to bring us down permanently and inhibit our love for life, we can grow from the experiences and use them to fuel our desire to joyfully become all we can be.

Value the Groundwork

Once our intention for joy is in place, it is important not to forget the groundwork. Intention is just part of the process. Understanding ourselves is also imperative. As human beings we all have fundamental needs that must be met, and they are basically the same. Beyond our physical needs we all want the same things: to feel a part of a larger community or movement, to know that we are not only competent but special, and to feel that our lives matter. Meeting these needs is something we consistently do, consciously or unconsciously, destructively or constructively. Don't forget to survey how you are fulfilling these needs. Are you expecting someone else to meet them for you? As long as we rely on someone else to rescue us, we won't feel the joy of self-esteem we could feel. Joy is always connected to our self-actualization.

The same is true of our personal beliefs about life. These beliefs are based on our unique experiences, and they determine the way we view the world and the way we react to events. Personal beliefs can create an environment that will support us as we strive to accomplish great things and have loving relationships. They can also limit us, especially when we have an unconscious belief that is in opposition to what we want in life.

Do a full inventory of your basic beliefs. Once you step back and examine the fundamental truths that are shaping your life, you can better determine if they are accurate and worth holding on to. Ask these kinds of questions: "What do I believe has to happen in a relationship in order for me to be happy?" "How will I know when I am successful?" This evaluation will help you develop a clearer vision of how you want your life to change. It will also lead you toward setting goals that reflect your heart's desires. As we discussed in Chapter Two, when we have a clear vision of our future, it is easier to stay in joy. We become excited about life and more alert to the opportunities around us.

It is important to keep our goals balanced and well rounded. If joy is our priority, then our goals shouldn't be just materialistic. It is important that they include relationships, health, and spirituality. And we need to consider the full reality surrounding our goals. If you want a new car, what will it mean financially? If you want to start a new business, how will that affect your relationships and free time? And if you want a lean, healthy body, how much time will you need to spend researching nutrition and working out?

Also be prepared to hang in there when the road to your goals gets a little bumpy. Stay steady, keep your eyes on the outcome, and be willing to shift your approach when necessary.

Write down your goals and review them regularly. This will help you nourish them by giving you a clear focus each day. It will also make your dreams more real. If you think about them routinely, you will develop more faith that they can come about.

Next, remember to prioritize your time and organize your space. No matter how much releasing of the past you accomplish or how much moving toward a brighter future you envision, until you organize your life, your progress will be slow. If you are always rushing around, cramming one more thing into your schedule, or if your surroundings are overflowing with papers and clutter, you aren't going to have the reflective time you need to stay alert and on top of your life events. Spend time following the steps outlined in Chapter Three. It will be well worth the effort.

Just as important in your journey toward greater joy is learning to communicate effectively with others. Once we start moving toward our goals and managing our time and surroundings, getting caught up in petty disagreements seems like a waste of time. Detecting control dramas and taking appropriate action to stay out of them is paramount. We know that people have different beliefs about life, which means there will be times when others won't agree with us. Always remember that in a disagreement people are coming from a different belief system, so don't take it personally. Figure out their point of view, and the communication will improve.

Live in the Mystery

Perhaps most important of all in maintaining a joyful attitude about life, as stated in Chapter Five, is learning to quiet our minds and cultivate a connection with the sacred. Here again our intention is necessary. We have to knock on the door and reach for the miraculous that lies beyond ordinary existence. Explore sacred sites, yoga, tai chi. Join a dance class, pursue the "zone" in various sports. Pray and explore your religious doctrines. In the end a connection with the sacred must be an experience, not just a good idea.

The same is true of quieting our minds. We must find ways to distract ourselves when we feel overwhelmed or overly concerned. Pay attention to the way foods you eat affect you emotionally. Capture your swirling thoughts on paper. And speak to yourself in a supportive way. Trust that a quiet mind is a possibility and believe it can be a part of your reality.

This is a necessary step in awakening to the truth that we are part of a bigger plan in life. Once we gain this awareness, events will begin to occur in our lives that carry a deeper mystery. You will find yourself marveling at information that seems to come at just the right time to bring your goals closer. Cultivate this sense of expectation.

Each morning begin with a primary question and then ask

yourself, "What mysteries will happen today to give me the answers I need?" Listen carefully to hunches and intuitions because they will move you into exactly the right spot for a synchronistic occurrence. Over time the miraculous events that happen will deepen your realization that something higher is guiding your life.

Your Life Is Important

You are part of a larger plan, and if you pay attention, you will realize that the guidance you experience is leading you in a particular direction. Each of us has a destined calling in life, a truth we must tell, one that becomes clearer as our lives proceed. Remember to spend as much time as necessary tracing your personal history. Look for clues and hidden meanings in all that has happened to you. Use this information, along with your strong desire to help make the world a better place.

Remind yourself that no truth is too small to be unimportant. In fact, the small truths, held with conviction and shared with everyone we meet, can be more effective than great projects. When you take the time to help one individual, and to communicate honestly and authentically, the effect cannot be measured. That person may go on to touch others and influence the world in a way that cannot be foreseen.

Real joy is secured when we pull all the pieces together into one conscious life journey that touches others and makes this world a better, more spiritual place. Remember that at the end of your life you want to look back and know you lived your time here with the greatest sense of awareness and purpose. Make joy a priority, and you will find levels of experience and satisfaction once thought unimaginable.

I would also like to thank the following people for allowing me permission to share their stories within: Jimmi Buell, Gloria Decker, Jerry Nelson, and Savann Sherrill. Thanks, also, to the National Association of Professional Organizers for allowing me to list contact information within.